D1124674

THE WRONG SEASON

The Wrong Season

JOEL OPPENHEIMER

THE BOBBS-MERRILL COMPANY, INC.
Indianapolis • New York

Some of this material appeared in a different form in The Village Voice.

The Bobbs-Merrill Company, Inc.
Indianapolis • New York

Copyright © 1973 by Joel Oppenheimer
All rights reserved
ISBN 0-672-51718-3
Library of Congress catalogue card number 72-89708
Designed by A. Christopher Simon
Manufactured in the United States of America

i spent all last night
        turnin' from side to side
spent all last night
        turnin' from side to side
now i was not sick
        i was just dissatisfied
            —*good mornin' blues*
                leadbelly

do what we can, summer will have its flies.
if we walk in the woods,
we must feed mosquitoes.
                    —*prudence*
                        emerson

this book is for
walter o'malley
and
gilbert sorrentino

ACKNOWLEDGMENTS

this book would not have been possible without the inspiration of larry merchant and pete hamill; the faith of gene rachlis; the openheartedness of vic ziegel; the cooperation of john dobbs; the advice of joe flaherty, philip bukberg, david wyland, bob smith, eddie hockey, and tommy sugar; the obduracy of norman marshall; the accuracy of david markson; the computer mind of don honig; the open eyes of jeanine johnson; the support of ross wetzsteon; the technical assistance of neal and matt barry keeping met records and michel dobbs as my yankee informant; the skill of brian breger; and the patience of helen oppenheimer.

to all of them, more thanks than are decent for more help than was proper.

INTRODUCTION

Baseball is the most democratic of games. Unlike football and basketball (and, in reverse snobbery, even the art of being a jockey), size has little to do with achievement and excellence. Indeed, when one thinks about it, baseball is the most humane game in existence.

Baseball rosters have included Three-Finger Mordecai Brown, One-Arm Pete Gray, and the wooden-legged pitcher, Monty Stratton. Which brings us full circle to Joel Oppenheimer. What other game would be loved by a poet with wall-to-wall bouffant hair who sexually assaulted a chicken in the film *The End of the Road*?

But then baseball is a game that attracts free spirits. Even the cliché of rooting for "the home team" is a lie, at least in my experience. My family lived in the heart of Brooklyn, a short peg from Prospect Park, a fungo away from Ebbets Field. Our house was hemmed in by the jangling parallels of trolley cars on McDonald and Coney Island avenues. Yet, with a father and four sons, not one Dodger fan was produced. When my old man arrived from County Galway, that tough-assed leprechaun John Mc-

Graw was ruling the roost at Coogan's Bluff. Thus, the Flahertys followed the green of the Metropolitan Transportation Authority to 155th Street and the Polo Grounds and became Giant fans forever.

Upstairs in our two-family house lived the O'Donnells. The sire, Paddy, pulled for the St. Louis Cardinals (they also had a goodly share of Celts). His oldest son, Tommy, rooted for the Chicago Cubs, because he suffered from some mystical affliction with Bill "Swish" Nicholson. The next son and my sidekick Joe—long before the terms "pragmatic" and "existential" became fashionable—rooted for any team that was five games out in front in late August.

Across the street in "The Hotel," a sprawling, wood-framed, multidwelling affair, lived Charlie Wright, a Yankee fan (even then we knew he was destined for the Dreyfus Fund), and Bobby Hampton, who, claiming 10 percent Cherokee blood, was a forerunner of Vine Deloria, as he chauvinistically war-whooped between the Indians of Cleveland and the Redlegs of Cincinnati.

So the young Yonkers Oppenheimer has to be forgiven for falling in love with the Dodgers of Brooklyn. What else could the poor child have done in those geographical circumstances—root endlessly for a trotter? Such was the dilemma of a tot born forty-five minutes from Broadway.

I met Oppenheimer about seven years ago in the Lion's Head Pub, when the *Village Voice* began to publish my work. Patrons gratuitously introduced him to me as "a poet." (What the hell did they think I thought he was—a weightlifter?) I soon realized I was in the company of a man of contradictions. He was a student of von Clausewitz, though he had never made the acquaintance of the Yonkers ROTC, and if you as much as touched him, he would call down the Geneva War Crimes Commission on you: "Goddammit, don't touch The Poet."

He was a Jew from Yonkers who drank bourbon with

the dedication of a Southern senior member of the House Ways and Means Committee. (A Roger Maris asterisk must be added here. *His liver is now back in the instructional league.)

I was also to learn that for a dude who wouldn't venture onto the West Side IRT he was an aficionado of the Old West. Indeed, on further perusal I found he had written a beautiful play about that period, titled *The Great American Desert*.

But my burly Brooklyn past wouldn't allow me to believe he was a baseball buff. Even when he showed me his school sweater with his letter emblazoned on it (for baseball, he claims; for iambic pentameter, I still swear) from Yonkers High, my street prejudice wouldn't allow it. Good God, the man's idea for a million-dollar infield was probably Pound to Eliot to Olsen. I was soon to learn that bourbon-bonded poets were harder to fathom than Rip Sewell's ephus ball.

Not only did he know the game, but his mind was as stacked with stats as Jane Russell's sweater in *The Outlaw*. I would receive phone calls at the most outlandish hours to answer his quizzes. The calls at midnight were bearable, but when Joel put the cork in the jug, like Billy Graham he thought the world had caught "the take sign" with him. So on mornings when my nerves were jumping away from my body, like Jackie Robinson off third, the phone would pound like the hammers of hell, and the voice would ask, "Who was the runner on third when Bobby Thomson hit the homerun in 1951?" I began to believe Joel was in the employ of either my parish priest or my mother.

When Macmillan published *The Baseball Encyclopedia*, he reacted like a lost soul who has found the original Torah in a train station locker. The quizzes became so esoteric I found myself frisking my own copy late into the night. Old arguments were rekindled: Who was the Lord of the Flies—Willie, Duke, Mickey? Who had been better—the awesome Yankees or the Dodgers of Reese, Robinson, Cox, Furillo, and Campanella? Since Oppenheimer had more industry at this sport than I, he usually beat my brains out.

But as Peter had his Rock, I had Bobby Thomson and the '51 Giants, a talisman against all Dodger history and accomplishment, the stigma that haunted the beloved Bums. When I waved this horror in front of him (which was perpetual), he would say very unpoetic things about my virility.

A sadness surrounded us though. His Dodgers and my Giants had gone the way of all flesh—to California. But like all poets, he had a touch of Charlie Brown in him, so he wrapped the Mets about him like a blanket. Cursed by an early addiction to the "true church," my heart remained in San Francisco with Willie. (Since Willie's return to New York, we are in cahoots, like Jesse and Frank; we've even gone to ball games together.) Joel's love and loyalty shouldn't be taken lightly, never mind his courage. Like the Flying Wallendas who mount the high wire after tragedy, Oppenheimer takes the subway to Shea Stadium in Queens.

The best was to come. Like a swain who couldn't control his heart anymore, he began to make his passion public in print. In a series of articles in the *Village Voice* he did some of the best quirky baseball writing in New York, thus the world, and, till we hear more from Houston Control, the universe. His work was laid out in box form, and one began to hear the term "the Oppenheimer box" among writers. Like that of all fine artists—Ted Williams' low-slung pants or the kick of Mel Ott's right leg—the Oppenheimer style became easily recognizable.

So, after touching the bases, he now brings us home with this book. The title is apt: *The Wrong Season.* Any reporter can write about winners; poets know how to plumb losers. And if truth has it, the Lord never equipped poets with a high hard one—the screwball is their metier.

Oppenheimer's penchant in that direction is one legions can swear by.

The season was wrong in many ways. The Mets were neither dynamic nor daffy, not comet or frizzler—God spare us the merely mediocre. Gil Hodges died, and memories of those prayers in Brooklyn many years ago for him to deliver a World Series hit were transformed into prayers for the delivery of his soul. When Jackie died, Joel lost an ancient god, and I felt as Grant must have felt when he accepted Lee's sword. As one ages, great adversaries are to be missed.

But with all this human failing, The Poet has pulled off a lovely book and rightfully so, since heartbreak is a poet's home park. But aesthetic honesty forces me to warn the reader to beware. Oppenheimer can lay down an aggravation as cunningly as Rizzuto dropped a bunt. And like his beloved Preacher Roe, he won't overpower you; but with his jiving, juking, and spit, he'll con you out of your pants.

His refusal to use capital letters is a case in point. The only way to account for his magic is to come to the conclusion that the wily old son of a bitch uses a foreign substance on his typewriter.

—JOE FLAHERTY

New York City

TWO BASEBALL POEMS

I

john g. "scissors"
mcilvain, described by
the sporting news as
remarkable, died
in charleroi, pa.,
recently. he was
88. he pitched for
22 minor league teams
in 15 different leagues
and was still in semi-
pro ball in his seventies.
when he won a 4–3 ball
game at seventy-five he
said: i don't see anything
to get excited about. i
think a person should feel
real good when he does
something unexpected.
i expected this. his
big disappointment was
that he never made the
majors, although he won
26 for chillicothe
one season, and 27 the
next. he was, however,
a bird-dog scout for
the indians for several
years. he had been
deaf since 1912.

II

andy the paperman at
bleecker and eleventh
is grungy, his paunch
and stubble offending
even me. he played
shortstop in the pennsylvania
league in 1941 and
believes "kids today
don't love the game
any more like we did."
he played against the
best of his time, major
leaguers and all, babe
dahlgren, sibby sisti,
you name 'em, he played
them all. he once
safely stole third through
a slough of mud, soaking
all through his shirt.

MY FATHER

my father was born in 1893. he was a new york giants fan. my son nathaniel was born in 1966. he is a new york mets fan. i was born in 1930 and i was a dodger fan and am a mets fan, and i hate the yankees. i have more self-confidence now, and have learned the virtues of passion, whether for or against.

my father, having switched to the mets with a desperation similar to mine, had problems devoting full energy to them because he had known the giants. but he was interested in rooting for and watching the national league, and they were the only national leaguers around, so they became his team. but i had twenty-five years of training with the dodgers, which meant i was able to take the mets to my bosom completely, from opening day in '62 on. his death came in August of '69, and so he never saw the pennant race, he never saw the series, and he never saw his grandson in a mets uniform. he did see me play on occasional visits to summer camp, where he watched as i hit texas leaguers from the three, four, or five slot and dropped a great many fly balls out in right field. maturity brought me the wisdom to move to the pitcher's mound, where the other guys are expected to do the fielding.

in any event, it occurs to me now that between the three, we've seen and will keep seeing the history of baseball, and that's a comforting thought. it lends a continuity to life which allows you to believe that the past really happened in a time when you ain't quite sure of it. john mcgraw was my father's motto, and i can't see he suffered by it. i, on the other hand, have always found something to bitch about with managers, although it took until just recently to get me mad at durocher.

well, what is this game? i'd like to think it is peculiarly "american," but i can't see any reason to do that aside from the empirical one that it grew up here and has few relatives anywhere else. it's a game in which time and space are warped into totally artificial limits, and i suppose that's part of it: games, after all, have always seemed to me to involve the suspension of reality so we can mess with a specific number of variables inside a rigid framework, thus getting away, for a little bit, from that hassle called life. well, by golly, it sure happens— sometimes so much that nothing happens. the dream is of a game that goes on and on, the last out never being made—or a batter fouling, fouling, fouling, so that no ball is ever fair and again the game goes on. thus time and space so carefully denoted are forever destroyed, or at least put on the shelf. i'm talking about that sag of spirit when you realize in the top of the ninth that you're five runs ahead and that unless the other team scores five the game will be over and you won't get to bat again. it happens to me whether i am playing or watching. *i want the game to go on.* that's an unrealistic view of the universe. every other game i can think of tells you when it's going to end either by an actual clock or by a defined

goal in points. in tennis they've even gotten dissatisfied
with that kind of end, so they have the tiebreaker. terrific.
if you want a game to end quickly why start it in the first
place? but baseball does more than take you out of time
and space, because it allows for a set of records and statistics that mean you don't even have to watch the game
to enjoy it. now that *is* wacky and american, i guess.
i mean there are guys who wouldn't go to a ball game if
you paid them, yet they are fans in the truest sense. al
koblin and wes joice own a bar where i hang out and
they won't let you turn a ball game on the house television, although i swear i've seen bowling matches on, on
slow days there, and yet neither of them can keep out of
a trivia war, or a favorite-all-time-team discussion, or a
day-by-day prognosis of the season. in horseracing if you
bet without at least thinking you know something about
the horse you're a fool, but baseball is constructed to let
everybody be a specialist. dave markson is my age, grew
up in albany watching kiner clout homeruns up there,
and can give you every batting average in both leagues
from 1935 to 1945. he hasn't seen a game since 1947, but
he's my consultant for "his" ten years. vic ziegel specializes
in the outré, so that when i wanted to know why jimmy
wilson caught an entire world series for the cincinnati
reds while they had ernie lombardi he gave me a complete dossier in ten minutes: lombardi sprained his ankle;
they reactivated wilson who was then past forty, and he
went on to be the hero of the series, with, among other
things, the only stolen base. you can't do this with any
other game, but then who would want to?

so my father told me about pie traynor, and i tell nathaniel about eddie mathews, and he, perhaps, will still
remember brooks robinson—he's only five and a half,
and we don't watch the american league at my house,
but perhaps he'll learn enough to lie about it, as we all
have. i say this because my own predilections have always

had to do solely with my team. i can talk for purposes of sociability about other players, other teams, and astonishing records, but in my heart the only thing that counts is my team and what it has done for me lately. with a history of dodgers and mets this is not easy, but it's the only way i know. in a secret place in my brain nobody ever played third base better than billy cox, but i have to prate on about mathews, since common sense does occasionally convince me that it's better not to get laughed out of the bar. this irrational loyalty allows me to enjoy every game because i am using standards no sane man could believe. sometime in february every year i work out two sets of statistics for the then-current mets squad: one set is their best-ever individual stats, the other is what my head tells me their lifetime averages ought to be. it is possible in this way to see eddie kranepool at .275 with twenty-two homeruns and eighty runs batted in, and i do, every february. and i have absolute faith that some september will prove me right. perhaps next year. you can see that i'm taking a mature view, though, since at thirteen i would have thought in terms of .300 and forty homers and one hundred rbis. i ask reasonable efforts from them all—although sometimes when i add up the number of wins and losses i've assigned the pitching staff it comes out to 180 games and i have to go back and refigure. for the 1972 season, for example, it looked like this:

seaver	26	8	
koosman	18	6	(i was convinced he was through with arm trouble)
gentry	18	8	(i had no faith in him, but much in his tools)
ryan	14	14	(remember, before the trade)
sadecki	6	1	(terrific if you spot him right)
mcandrew	4	3	(oh ye of little faith)
williams	6	2	(before willie)

taylor	6	2	(i assumed a lot of work for the relievers)
frisella	9	2	
mcgraw	11	2	
	118	48	

so that i had four games over, but i couldn't honestly take any away except from taylor, frisella, and mcgraw. you see that i was trying to be realistic—i mean every one of those guys *could* do what i put him down for. that they didn't isn't terribly important, and i will figure it again and again, every season. and there are bonuses— in february of 1970 i discovered that our pitchers had an overall winning record lifetime for the first time since the mets began. that carried me through april.

you will note that i had not figured ryan to really contribute; that is, my assumption was that he could win big one day and blow it in the first inning five days later, but that there was nothing to do but keep him in the rotation. so you have to believe me when i say that i did not mind the trade. i minded the way fregosi ended up between injuries and sporadic hitting and fielding, but i thought all along that ryan was the expendable pitcher. i didn't like giving up stanton—that's who i didn't like in that trade. i'm still not convinced that ryan could make it for the mets, considering the bombing of '71—i really think he had too many problems with this club, and i wonder too about whether he isn't the kind of pitcher who can make it in the american league but not in the national. i mean i believe the line that high fastballs work over there and they don't here, but again i believe that because i want to, and i refuse to do any research to find out whether it's indeed true or not. the game allows and in fact demands that sometimes. the big mistake of course was mcandrew, but since the met management made that mistake also, that will be my cop-out. i mean, it was sometime in august when they told us that san diego would have given us colbert for gentry and we offered mcandrew. oh wheel of fortune . . . because of course what we all said about mcandrew was if they traded him, where would we get that one win in september? so i have to say that it was with genuine embarrassment that i started complaining in june that gentry was still in the rotation and mcandrew wasn't. it wasn't only that gentry kept failing, but that mcandrew did make us all believers.

but i was in february and here i am now in june, and that's not fair. in fact i was in 1893, but time zooms and is arbitrary in a book as well as baseball, and i can't stop to worry about it. the fact is that ernie lombardi lying stretched out by homeplate is inextricably messed up in my head with harrelson and milner crashing in left field, and all disasters and victories blend into one somehow. nathaniel understands this way of thinking very well, so i presume we'll be able to watch baseball games together for the next several years at least. my second oldest son, daniel, sixteen, on the other hand, spent the summer of '70 here and drove me crazy calling aspromonte an old man, and rooting for lou brock of all people. he claims he is a mets fan too, but i'd like to see him at home in new mexico and see who he really roots for. his mother, who was from north carolina, has remained as far as i can tell a charley choo-choo justice fan if anything. my oldest son, nicholas, eighteen, is now at college, and between open dorms and so on, is not, i believe, terribly interested in spectator sports any more.

but i'm forty-two, and the doctor won't let me drink any more, and i'm in terrible shape, so i'm back with baseball. i know, i know, there are healthy people watching too, but i like it my way, because it's obvious looking at me that spectating is my only choice. but what they don't know is that in those glorious days when i *was* participating, from those dropped flies at camp wah-kee-nah, through being the best second-string tackle at yonkers high school up to and including my seventeen-and-five season with the poets and painters protective association league in '65, i always looked like this. i was always in terrible shape, and i can't blame it on the booze. it's my soul, or perhaps my stars.

in any event i was searching for possible titles for this book and i garbled a quote. i kept thinking of shakespeare: now is the summer of our discontent, and finally i went and hauled out richard the three and there it was, only for some strange reason it said *winter*. oh well, you win a couple, you lose a couple, and this certainly has been the summer of my discontent, and there it is. because now is the summer, all the time. winter is the time you think about it, huddled too cold for anything else. winter sports are something they thought up so they could get all sweaty and make believe it was the summer. even if it was the wrong season.

PRE-SEASON

1

when nathaniel got back from his grandma's he announced that new york was terrific and he sure hated long island and that ranked only with his asking david once, on church avenue in brooklyn on a lovely sunday afternoon as they walked toward the aquarium, what country is this?

i got worried but when i asked him about the visit it turned out it was really only long island and not grandma he was mad at. in fact he was very excited because he and the nabel boy—and i was afraid to ask him if the neighbors were named nabel, or if that was someone who lived next door—had played baseball. the other kid was the red sox and he was the mets. the mets won 8–1. he also said he almost hit one out of the yard. the yard is fifteen by forty but i don't know where homeplate was.

he was five and a half at his first contact with the ball. i was seven, at camp wah-kee-nah, and it was a light tap to the mound. nobody was terribly supportive, it being

1937 and a nonprogressive camp. as a matter of fact black and blue marks on the arm from raps by the counselors were badges of pride. i once lost sixty-two desserts out of obduracy, saying yassuh, massa, to artie ferrante sixty-three times in a row. the first one only got the warning. but i kept playing baseball.

by thirteen i was catching and batting cleanup and was once walked intentionally four times in a row, the other camp having heard about me. in desperation my fifth time at bat i golfed a low and outside 3&0 pitch into right center for a two-run scoring triple. i was never much of a pull hitter, my best shot ever being a sweet clean line drive going through between left and center and rolling, rolling, rolling.

the fatal flaw was my fielding, and since i spent only one season in relative obscurity behind the plate, it was very fatal indeed. i was once responsible for all the runs in an 8–7 ball game, knocking in five, scoring three, and dropping two fly balls and booting one grounder for their seven.

so when i was twenty i turned myself into a pitcher. by then we were playing softball but i still couldn't field. as i've mentioned i was a junkman. i had a knuckleball, perhaps the only one in softball, a slider which i threw off one knuckle, an ephus that sometimes crossed the strike zone, a straight slow ball, a medium speed pitch that had nothing and unless timed and placed exquisitely invariably went for a homerun, and a sizzling fast ball that once in fifteen years was caught by the catcher for a strike. it went under over through and around him the rest of the time. from thirty to thirty-three or so i was in therapy with a marvelous guy. he promised me when he finished i would have a fast ball, but it never happened. but, since he delivered in other areas, i guess i shouldn't complain.

the apex of my career was a short stint with a semi-professional club in new hampshire—one of those leagues supported by local merchants, with a money prize and a trip for the league leaders and nothing for the rest. i arrived to go to work in a print shop at eleven on a monday, threw a ball around at lunch that day with one of the other young printers, was signed as a pitcher that night, and started the next for the kendall insurance team. we were in last place due to a nonexistence of pitchers, although the team fielded and hit fairly well. i threw a little monday night, and a little tuesday at lunch. i was twenty-three and already out of shape. tuesday night with a little bit of luck, like they say, i won 7–5. friday night i went again and won 3–1. tuesday following i threw a shutout, and the next friday we won again. after the third tuesday game i not only had a five and o record, but the weekly paper had my name in the head-line, small but nevertheless a head: kendall moves up, oppenheimer wins fifth. the sixth game was against the league leaders. the first guy up bunted, and i threw wild past first. the second guy bunted and i flubbed it. men on first and third. five bunts and four runs later with the bases loaded and no outs and seven errors on me i be-came a pinchhitter for the rest of the season.

and until my great season with poets and painters pro-tective association south of washington square park, where i rang up the 17–5 record including three sunday iron-man stunts, that was it. fortunately i had the good sense to retire after that season and am now available only for the throwing out of first balls around the village. two years ago i did indeed branch out by attempting the ceremonial opening center jump in a basketball game be-tween the lion's head and max's kansas city, but i won't try that again.

the baseball maxims i have lived by include lefty gomez's one about clean living and a fast friendly outfield, and satch's advice never to look behind you because someone may be catching up. i always tried to meet the ball when batting and throw low and to the corners when pitching, although quite often it worked out the other way.

2

the worst sin a father can commit with his son, as everyone including me keeps telling me, is to try to lay your
imprint on him, telling him who to root for, what to like,
what to want to be or do. well, i just been asitting here
watching the television set, and somehow nathaniel is
turning into a mets fan. it's true that i made his best
friend take off his yankee cap when he came in the
house, but that was just joking. except that joshua believed me and hasn't worn it since. he also doesn't bad-
mouth the mets to nathaniel too much any more, so how
big a sin could it be?

but there are other problems. the other day one of the
kids in the building, an eighteen-year-old whose folks i
had known back when he was three, came by. he has a
genuine mets uniform and it was nathaniel's size. it was
a real flannel job, too, not cheap acetate, and it had obviously stood up to many a washing, since it was faded
but in good shape. nathaniel had it on and off sixteen
times in an hour, putting it on to trot down the hall to

show it to norman, back, out of it, into it again to show claire, etc., etc., etc. but then when he got dressed to go downstairs, he put on his old t-shirt and his ripped corduroys. aren't you going to wear the uniform? i'm afraid the yankee fans'll laugh at me, he said.

well, yankee fans never change, as i hope to make abundantly clear, but in the meantime we had a problem here of peer acceptance or whatever the term is. so we had a long talk about how difference of opinion made for horseraces and ball games and how people might tease you, but you just teased them back, and how if someone said the mets were yuk to tell them the yankees were yuk. he went downstairs in his torn corduroys and his t-shirt. of late he has taken to saying that he likes the yankees but he loves the mets . . . which is a subtle difference but a terrific approach to life which it took me three years of emotional counseling to arrive at, so i guess he's way ahead of the game. of course my problem wasn't baseball teams. so i have laid this terrible burden on him in a terrible season. have there ever been this many major injuries on one club? i doubt it. first the outfield's wiped out, then the infield's gone, and even seaver gets a pull in his gluteus maximus. i don't want to cry, because like the man said, you cry alone.

but then i started out crying, at age seven or eight or so, taken to a game at the polo grounds by the jewish community center of yonkers. there were maybe thirty or forty of us kids and they were all giant fans. so of course i became a dodger fan. and the dodgers lost the first game 26–3. and that was the beginning of it. in '41 at age eleven i heard mickey owen drop the third strike as i walked up park hill avenue going to see aunt gus and uncle morris. year after year with the brooks, the long hauls and the disappointments and the big ones coming too late—and even damned in my choice of heroes: don newcombe who could turn every team in both leagues

8

upside down but couldn't do it to the yankees; duke snider playing behind mays and mantle; campanella hurt before we could really show the yankees he was better . . . and on and on.

so i take my own kid at age five and a half, ready and ripe for it, and i think i'm handing him a winner, and the whole damned team goes to the hospital. he'll live through it, but will i? and i suppose i will, like any good new york fan this year. i mean, after all, it really didn't matter who or what you followed between willis reed's knee and namath's thumb and the ranger injuries and the mets losing melchionni in the play-offs, not to mention the giants removing themselves to jersey. i'm sure i forgot some because if ever there was a city born to die the hard way this is it. so nathaniel might as well learn it early.

but i'm sure you noticed that the summer of '72 was also a terrible season for watching any baseball team with any kind of loyalty. we had the presidential conventions, a world championship match in chess, and the olympics. chris schenkel never tired of telling me that there were over sixty hours of network time on the games and i logged damned near fifty of them. i tried from time to time to follow the mets on the radio while the set was on, but the olympics ain't like other sports, since you have to pay attention to know when the color commentary stops and the coverage begins.

the conventions shouldn't have interfered, god knows, but somehow they did. i rationalized it by seeing both of them as giant sports events, even if i knew the end results. i mean the democrats were the sixties' mets and the republicans were the always yankees. but you have to keep score, nevertheless.

instances of how bad it was this summer follow: we were invited out for the opening night of the democratic convention. we went over to mary breasted's place, mary being a writer for the *village voice*, and aside from me, probably the only one of the *voice* writers who wasn't in miami covering something. i don't know what her excuse was, but i had applied for the rights to stassen's headquarters and had been turned down. my second option was harry truman's bedside. my thinking was that if it really was time for a change one or the other might sneak in on the thirtieth ballot, but the *voice* wouldn't buy either idea. in any event mary was in new york so she threw a convention party, and we were in new york so she invited us. with a ten-month-old baby in the house you would even be willing to go to a rockefeller-for-president party if it gets the two of you out of the house. but the problem was that the mets had a game with san francisco at the same time, and it followed our disastrous 1–2 series with both san diego and los angeles. i still had delusions that we would straighten out, and, quite frankly, i had foreseen at least a 7–2 record against the three west coast clubs in this stand. a sweep of san francisco would at least have made it 5–4, so when we arrived and found that we were the first of the expected guests i didn't allow myself any qualms about asking mary if i could watch the game until the people came. there was a young man wandering about but he seemed to be a friend there to help. he turned out later to be an acquaintance there to score points, but that's not my problem. anyhow, she said sure, although he bristled, and when i explained to him i was thinking about doing a book about the mets he allowed as how i could watch if i wanted to. of course, when the people came, there were a couple of remarks from him, now that he had an audience, about over-aged baseball fans, but you get used to that. i didn't understand the over-aged anyhow because it seems to me that watching baseball is one of the pleasures of old age, and i have remarked often on the proximity of one of the scharf retirement homes to shea stadium. it seems to me that if my kids chip in and get me one of those aluminum walkers i could probably leave at ten or so with a brown-bag lunch and make all the old timers' days, admission fifty cents. i watched an inning or so with nothing happening and then the guests came and we switched to the convention.

after an hour of the hassling i searched out mary's clock-radio, and after checking with her so she'd know it was mis-set and wouldn't wake up in terror the next morning when bruce bennett came blaring out, i kept sneaking in to pick up the score. the mets blew it and i heard every minute of horror, walks and errors and hits. now you can do that sort of thing properly but not if you're expected to be paying attention to the convention. if i had been home, just screwing around at the set and checking in on my own radio, it would have been different. but we lost to san francisco the next night too.

on the other hand the philly double-header i squeezed in at my brother's fiftieth birthday party worked out splendidly. not only did we win two, but koosman hit somebody hard enough to bruise him and i figured his fastball was coming back. that one, since it was family, was easy. they're still hoping i'll become a dean or doctor or something, but writing a book about baseball seems infinitely preferable to them if it's a choice of that or poetry. so when we walked in my brother said we won the first game—the we being puzzling since he was always the yankee fan. given that opening i looked him straight in the eye and asked him where the television set could be put so i could watch the second game. understand that there were approximately one hundred and twenty west-chester doctors and wives milling about the house at that point. he told me that the color set was in their bedroom and i'd find chairs and ashtrays and everything ready. that was terrific. especially since i couldn't drink, which, i'm embarrassed to admit, is the way i've made it through most such gatherings. this meant we were now allowed to mingle and split, mingle and split. it was a lovely party. it was really only marred by the fight i had with helen because i told my brother that she had to watch with me to take notes for me. she claimed that this was male-chauvinist nonsense, turning her into a secretary, as if she couldn't do anything else. i admitted it was. after all why else would she watch a ball game? and would she rather be out in the party alone? no, she wouldn't, but i think she was plumping for status as co-author. non-writers always think being a writer is status. wives of writers should really know better. the second game ended just as the food was served. it was terrific timing. this ploy for surviving difficult social situations can be used only occasionally, however, which is too bad.

the fischer-spassky matches also killed a couple of day games and all the sundays, but i couldn't resist shelby lyman and his offstage expert edmar, so i had to stay with them. the problem is that you keep getting touted by these other things because deep in your soul you believe that nothing irrevocable happens in a ball game, but it might in conventions or other sports. the belief about baseball is of course true, but it's equally true that nothing irrevocable happens with the other stuff either. did i really need to watch mark spitz? i would, i suppose, have liked to watch larry young or frank shorter, but they just showed you pieces of the long races. that was dumb.

spencer holst lives across the hall from me. he's my age, he's small, he's a poet. but his father used to be a sports-writer for the detroit times and every spring of his child-hood spencer got carried off to that magic world of spring training. this was the early thirties, remember. in 1934 the tigers won the pennant with greenberg, gehringer, goslin, and cochrane, and they repeated in '35. that must have been a hell of a training camp. spencer hates base-ball.

nevertheless it seems to me it's the dream of the rest of us to be in florida in february—not miami beach, heavens, but tampa or st. pete or fort lauderdale, wher-ever you can run around pounding the old glove while the winter muscles loosen in that warm sun. oh yeah! and we read the papers while the sleet comes and comes, and we keep tucking our heads in and walking into the wind.

so this year i was going to do it. in december i talked

about it in the bar, by january i had helen ready to pack, and then february appeared and i was under the gun.

THIRTY-SEVEN OR SO REASONS FOR NOT GOING TO ST. PETERSBURG

1. trouble in flight. bomb threats. hijacks—a rash of them just this last week, all on flights to florida. none on tampa flights, but why not?
2. the primary results. why inflame further a populace which gave over fifty percent of its vote to wallace and jackson? especially in st. pete, which is composed primarily of older, more conservative voters interested in stability to begin with. i do have a scraggly beard and long hair.
3. general fear of traveling. my once-useful shrinker used to say it had to do with not being able to make it on public transport. he meant sexually. it now occurs to me that i wouldn't like trips even if we had a 1946 nash rambler with seats that folded into beds at the touch of a finger "for hunting and fishing trips" you bet!
4. sickness. helen has a terrible cold which she caught from nathaniel, who has bronchitis and is on one of the cillins and a codeine-based cough medicine which we had to hide from our dinner guests the other night, since if there is one thing i've learned, it's not to trust 1950's junkies even if they're ex. lemuel's nose has been running for two days and while he has no fever he's obviously working on his first cold. not really something to take pictures for the grandparents about, but we'd worry, wouldn't we? i've grown an abscess where my neck meets my chest and i'm on antibiotics too, and the doctor's going to have to lance it and watch it drain, he says. i thought it was a carbuncle, which nathaniel called carbumple, which made me feel better about it, but the doctor says carbumples have several heads, boils have one head, and this is an abscess because it has no heads. skeats says: a gathering of humors into one place and that it comes from the latin, literally "a going away."
5. to prove i don't really need the trip to do the book. everybody doesn't understand that i'm not covering the team—i

suppose i could say i'm covering me covering the team so that anything goes, but in fact what fan ever went to spring training? the whole point now that i think of it is to sit around the house thinking about how nice it must be down there, watching occasional clips on tv news and reading the paper every day, and figuring out the schedule: which games one might go see, thinking about going to montreal on the weekend of july fourth to see four games up there, working out dave schneck's complete minor-league slugging average (well over .600—i believe the first time we've ever had that, anywhere in our chain), and trying to work out the year's rotation if everyone is healthy and good.

6. general fear of new places. how will i go to sleep in a hilton hotel in st. petersburg? merchant already scared the shit out of me telling me of the joys of watching a game from the roof of al lang field, looking over tampa bay. i get acrophobia up behind homeplate at shea!

7. general fear of new people. hodges is a square. everybody says it, the squares proudly, everybody else, to explain why he don't understand cleon, and why tug had to shave off his moustache first day of training. the front office is probably worse. so despite their obvious kindnesses over the phone, what would they do when they saw me in the flesh? it's better to save that for my own turf, here in the city.

8. book parties. three in two days, at which i did manage to talk to jackie robinson, see two arms and one leg while the lady wrestlers wrestled, and have several ginger ales drinking at the players' club bar surrounded by portraits of john drew and edwin booth, and the like, all of whom seemed to be sneering at me. john drew was a beautiful man, and i wanted to write a play for him immediately if i had the time. these book parties were scheduled right in the middle of the best possible time to see the club, so that any later date would not be a true gauge of where the mets were, of and by themselves, and vis-à-vis their competition.

9. bad-weather reports from florida. in fact the first game scheduled to be televised from down there was rained out. who needs that when we had thunder-snowstorms up here?

10. reassessment of fiscal position, leading to the decision that the trip would put me in unnecessary financial bind, and

since the trip was, as outlined in 5, unnecessary for the book, why go? thinking like this does not produce investigative reporting and i will never really know about seaver's arm. but then, the doctors won't either. in the end, march is for sitting home warming up, damn it, and not for gallivanting around!

march 5th

the point with the sporting news as with any trade journal is to look at it only occasionally, because in this way you stay with it—each feature becomes something new, and the columnists don't grow stale. i mean people keep raving to me about *women's wear daily*—how it's got great theater coverage, some terrific writers, insights you wouldn't believe—but the idea of reading every issue is one of the most depressing prospects conceivable. so, when i made the paper run sunday morning and saw the spring-training issue of baseball's bible sitting right next to the *times*es and *news*es i picked it up—the first televised exhibition game was on that afternoon, and what a terrific way to start the season! what i didn't know was that it was raining in florida and that jim fregosi would break his thumb during that rain while infield practice went on before a game that wouldn't be played. talk about portents—the trade was bollixed already, before ryan threw one pitch in anger, before anyone had even had a chance to bitch about the failure of our forty-sixth starting third baseman.

when the rain-out was announced, with me sitting poised expectantly in my easy-chair, nathaniel playing outside, lemuel being kept quiet by helen, then there was no damned thing left to do but read the damned paper from cover to cover. i read the columns, the predictions, the editorials, the letters, and i even read the ads, and that's what saved the sunday:

the new england patriots
offer for sale
7,000-seat grandstand

for the first time in my life, or maybe the second or third, i wanted to be rich, filthy rich, so rich i could pick up the phone and dial 617-269-7200 and ask for mr. john p. karle of the marr scaffolding company. "hi, john," i'd say. "listen, i saw your ad in the *sporting news* . . ."

like the ad says this "same seating would cost in excess of $150,000 in today's market," and the marr people do offer "expert advice and assistance in arranging for layout, in-stallation, etc.," and there was a combination built-in press box and/or covered seats at the top of the grand-stand where maybe i could put in those magic boxes like the garden is offering so you can combine the live arena and the comfort of your living room. this package, on such a day, seemed to me ideal, and it was only $55,000, fob weston, massachusetts. the whole idea of "free on board" has intrigued me since junior high school where we cov-ered it along with other handy business abbreviations. i mean, just how much would it cost you to get it any-where from weston, mass.? and yet the *free* was always the magic word that suckered me. i suspect i could be conned into buying an elephant if the price sounded like a bargain and it was fob anywhere.

but this fob had more intriguing implications. it all sounded so temporary and portable that i wondered if you just drive up in a volksbus and carry it away? would the vw advertising agency be interested? george lois would have bought it, back at the beginning, i know, and i could have been on television night after night, stowing my grandstand and collecting a check, fifty-two dollars every time it ran, norman tells me. and mr. karle, too, right there helping me fold it up, or deflate it, or whatever the hell you do with a seven-thousand-seat grandstand fob weston massachusetts.

and it wouldn't be a pig in a poke, either, or factory seconds, or "like new," not with the patriots. the description of its condition read: "excellent—used for just six days per season for three seasons." i could almost hear mr. karle adding in dulcet tones that for those eighteen days it was sat on by little old ladies from the finer sections of boston, back bay included, ladies who didn't jump up and down. in fact, it may never even have been sat on by anybody, but i don't have the patriots' home-attendance figures handy.

the afternoon reveries led on—the competition might be fierce with added starters in the bidding. for one thing, nixon was about to go off on the moscow trip, and given the reception when he came back from china, he might want the stand for the airport, to add both a touch of law and order, and a taste, even so faintly, of his beloved football. cheerleaders, ushers, souvenir butchers, the whole thing, all could be done beautifully, and there was that press box way up on top, where the fourth estate could be properly sequestered.

or the giants might be interested, given wellington mara's problems with yankee stadium and the jersey swamps not yet being ready. he could pick this thing up at this bargain price, keep it stuffed in *his* volksbus, and haul it around to wherever they decided to play. it might even fit at sixth avenue and twenty-fifth street—there used to be a pretty fair playground there that we used for softball. it could fit nicely right in sixth avenue, and what with light sunday traffic it wouldn't even be in the way.

any newspaper could use it, so its people could grind their favorite axes in public. the *news* could hold giant spelling bees, and the *times* could display the one hundred neediest cases. if the *voice* bought it, fred morton could be thrown to his fellow jews week after week, and fran lee and clark whelton could circle dogs as the dogs circled them, and mary nichols could take on the "wrong" reformers, while joe flaherty took on the "right" reformers. jill johnston could erect in public as well as in print.

the very word *print* opens new possibilities: clifford irving doing his research while all those people watched! nina van pallandt a star even quicker! howard hughes using it for his next closed-circuit call! the mind, as it so often wants to, truly boggles.

but while it boggles, it wonders whether this ad represents just another example of good old american free enterprise. can it be that simple? or is it really deeper, more nefarious? is it, maybe, another plot by the ecofreaks, who want, as everyone knows, to recycle everything? last week i heard jeffrey st. john compare nixon's trip to china to chamberlain's sell-out at munich. shouldn't the stands, then, be sold to russia for scrap to be made into missiles?

in the meantime, simple arithmetic shows that the stand breaks down to about eight bucks a seat, which makes a box worth thirty-two dollars. that's a very reasonable price for a christmas gift these days, and it doesn't need batteries—but would they consider selling it piecemeal like that? i suspect not, and i think the little guy is being shut out again, in speculating as well as agriculture and car manufacturing.

which last leads inescapably to the conclusion that this entire meander by me is a vaguely hidden radic-lib attack on the fiber of america, and it can't be allowed to continue. because now i'm thinking questions like: will the cars ever be able to get to the *new* patriots stadium and use the *new* seats there? my cousin lives in natick, maybe twelve miles away from foxboro, and he tells me the cars were stacked up in front of his house last season. maybe those seats, hardly used also, will be up for sale next year. for that matter, why did they need seven thousand more seats (easily expandable to ten thousand) in fenway anyhow? who came to see the games? does ted williams know about this? does ted williams care?

and if all this happens to me when the mets cancel an exhibition game and lose a third baseman, what's in store for the rest of the season, who, like they say, the race heats up? oh, if i had only known when i wrote that back in march, i would've stayed with the ads in the *sporting news*, and never, ever, watched a game all season long.

it's become increasingly chic to be involved in things like astrology, tarot, mind trips, and the like, and everybody and his brother has a good scientific reason, drawn from his favorite anthropologist or sociologist or shrinker as to why we're doing it, and why it's natural at a time like this, and how it can or can't hurt us. all i can say for myself is that the calendar has always been terribly important to me, and i tend to believe that holidays, for example, mean something, and exist for reasons. so when i looked at the calendar a few weeks ago and realized that easter, passover, and april fool's day were going to fall together this year, i decided it would have something to say about spring. indeed, along came the baseball strike, gil hodges' death, and roy campanella's rehospitalization.

a quick check with my resident astrologer, just to see if the stars as well as the calendar said anything, showed saturn and mars conjuct in gemini opposite neptune in sagittarius.

that was fine, but when i asked the resident astrologer what it told her she dove into an hour-long consultation with her familiar, and then the both of them spent forty-five minutes trying to explain their conclusions to me. i'm not blaming them, but something definitely got lost in translation. what i end up with then is what i understand of what they told me as reinforced by my poet's sense of metaphor. i see foot-dragging impetuosity in the real world, opposing pure idealism laced with rank fantasy in the world of philosophy otherwise known as games. or, in other words, total schizophrenia all around.

well, the television coverage of the beginning of the strike essentially supported this thesis. back at the ranch, in winter haven, a roving camera found some old codgers hanging around the ball park waiting for an exhibition game that wouldn't be played.

they said things like "it isn't fair," "they (the players) are spoiled," and, best of all, "why are they striking now, in the baseball season?"

i've heard this question many times during strikes, like the cabdriver asking me ten years ago why the newspapers went on strike just before christmas, when the people needed to see the ads for christmas shopping. but i guess people who spend their old age in retirement in the sunshine state on pensions won in union fights in the thirties don't ever muse on the theory of labor action, and it obviously would've fit in better with their plans and interfered less with their pleasure if the baseball players had gone out in december. i'm not mad at them, but rather at all of us.

predictably, the papers up here took off in defense of american ideals, but there was a big bonus. dick young used his news column for the strike for a while and laid off black athletes. he really couldn't blame this one on them, but he used the opportunity to transfer his venom to unions in general. somewhere along the way he dropped what has to be my favorite line when, after quoting marvin miller, the players' attorney, to the effect that a surrender at this point would see the destruction of the players' association, young said, "these are tired clichés used by every cajoling labor organizer since the abolition of the sweat shop." i'm sure everybody knows, as mr. young obviously does, that the sweat shop was the only abuse of the workers ever perpetrated by the bosses, and that the idea was dropped by the bosses themselves, of their own volition, because they discovered that it was a bad thing.

honestly, dick! i mean there are lots of arguments to make these days about a strike, and even about labor organizers—vide: every time albert shanker gets up on his hind legs and talks about the misery of being a teacher in new york city—but it is, after all, 1972, and baseball is, after all, a business.

but the news did balance his column with the loveliest of headlines and i thank them for that. across the spread it read: no game today; houk bewildered. i can see ralphie now. he's at the ball park, he has his glove, he looks bewildered indeed. and, monday, three days into the strike, phil pepe wrote a column for them, writing a little scared it seemed to me, as if maybe young were looking over his shoulder, allowing as how maybe, just maybe, the players were being bum-rapped. that maybe the continual citing of the "average" thirty-grand-a-year pay-check, with no mention of the "average" four-and-a-half-year career—and no mention of the few players whose salary brings that average up—might just be telling one side of the story. sure, i find it hard to bleed for a yo-yo jock making a lot of money for playing a game, but if i had to choose i'd rather bleed for them than phil wrigley or cbs, you betcha. i been saying for a long time that nobody ever went to the stadium to watch connie mack wave his scorecard around.

those owners keep talking about how they're doing it for me, how the players are going to destroy the game. i think they don't understand something. baseball will survive or die through the kids, like with any other game. if the kids play it, get turned on by it, then we'll have baseball. if they start playing football or soccer or pool instead, and don't care about baseball, baseball will die.

the loveliest statement of this came from larry merchant, who covered opening day as usual: in the east river park, central park, washington square—anywhere kids were throwing a ball around, taking cuts, choosing up sides. he was right. the only fans who would get screwed by the disappearance of "professional baseball" are the same ones who get upset when phosphates get declared illegal and they think they're being discriminated against. they appear on television newscasts and scream about their god-given right to be clean even if it means destroying the universe. i heard one lady say that this way: "i don't care about their water, my clothes are going to be clean!" and the connection is there, too, because they are same kind of people who think baseball consists of multicolored panels on the facade of shea stadium, or moving pictures of the stars on an exploding scoreboard. these people will indeed get screwed, because they've either forgotten or never knew how the heel of the hand ached after that first march day of throwing the ball around—and when they get hold of a signed baseball to give to their kid they yell at him if he plays with it, but he knows what a base-ball is for.

there *was* one argument this week that i couldn't handle. i stopped in murray's for the organic, natural, fertile, large, fresh eggs for the week and i heard the radio tuned to wins in the background and when the sports news came on, just as murray's wife was starting to wait on me i said hold it a minute, i want to hear if anything's happening with the strike. murray went into an old leftist scream about rich athletes, and opiates of the people, and when i tried to explain why i was backing the strikers he and his wife looked at me sadly and broke, in unison, into a marvelous parody of "when i grow too old to dream" that started "when i get too old to fight i'll become a trotskyite." why supporting the players association made me a trotskyite i don't know, but i walked around for two weeks with the song in my head.

the other thing that had been in my head before the strike was still rattling around there too and that was the season itself, because the last week of the exhibition schedule is when you start that kind of figuring, and i couldn't drop it now, just because there might not be a season.

i mean, that's the week you go to bed secure in all sorts of beliefs: like the exhibitions don't count, except the ones you've won, and that batters who aren't hitting now will start to, while the batters who are hitting are obviously raring to go already, and the pitchers are ahead of the batters anyway and *your* pitchers are going to stay that way. will seaver ever lose? i doubt it, or at least not before the all-star break. then too, the schedule is favorable, because a preliminary check shows that the mets can't lose a game until, possibly, the sag of jetlag in l.a. at the end of april. and that'll only be the first one of the three-game set that they drop. and since it's clear that the mets will run away with the season, you settle down quiet nights with the macmillan encyclopedia and the baseball register, and you update records to see who has a shot at what.

clemente needed nine triples to make the top twenty-five triples hitters of all time. he didn't make it—he got only seven in 1972 and won't hit any more. it ain't funny— because musial is the only modern on the list, and he's got a lot more at-bats, so that's nice select company for one of our boys to be in. i mean, hardly no one hits triples these days.

despite the fact that henry aaron is becoming everybody's darling, and fickle fame has turned her glance away from willie, because of the damned homeruns, henry is still worthy of attention, because he's moving up on a lot more than that. like, this season, he should move to second in all-time hits, runs batted in, and total bases, as well as making the homerun run.

hoyt wilhelm can't really gain anything, since he leads in practically all the categories he can lead in anyhow, but ain't it a groove that he's still going at forty-eight, turning forty-nine?

tom seaver needs thirty-five wins to pass christy mathewson's total for his first six years, and he and nancy need just one more commercial to give me spasmodic nausea.

cleon jones needs to bat .375 with five hundred at-bats to have a lifetime .300 average. his middle name is joseph.

and understand that this is what baseball's about, too— this and the kids. so when you laugh at me, hunched over my transistor at the dark end of the bar, laugh quietly. remember that i don't laugh at you as you stare at the greater greensboro open, whatever that may be. i know that ken sobol, alone in front of his stromberg-carlson on memorial day, dazed by all the radio-borne static of all those growling offenhausens, understands. i

know that tommy sugar in the rain at aqueduct understands. and i know that the reasonable world does not.

the hope is eternally there—always some specific hopes;
this year, before the strike, it was to see vida sign, to see
that fast ball rip through. it was even to wish that bou-
ton's knuckler kept floating through the jersey night,
just like his fast ball once cut through october days, and
to hope that nathaniel learned once and for all the right
way to hold a bat—he's five and a half, and give me a
child 'til he is six, i ain't got much time—and then, the
constant hope, the thing the game is about, the moments
of perfection in the long, slow drag of the game, the long,
slow drag of the season. i wanted to see those.

now i have to worry, instead, if willie, poor willie, can
keep his legs for one more season if i don't see him this
one.

and the owners? well, they worry about things like where
to put your favorite ball club when they take it away, and
what color to make the uniforms this year to attract the
ladies, or what kind of unopenable plastic bag to put the
mustard in. ballplayers play ball, on the other hand. they
understand as well as eight-year-olds playing monopoly
the laying down of arbitrary rules on a nonexistent grid
of the universe.

what it comes to, despite the public proclamations, is that
the owners have taken their ball and gone home, and so,
like always, we'll have to stuff a sock and bat it around if
we want to play.

or suppose we got bill veeck to form a new league? one
where, say, new york city owned the ball club and the
profits did us all some good? but that, mr. young would
say, smacks of socialism, and besides, since the abolition

of the poorhouse, there's nothing wrong with society any more, right? all i can say is, while my soul lusts for the season like a politician lusts for november, nevertheless: off the bosses! up the players! no god, no master, one big union!

the strike wasn't the only thing that happened, because
gil hodges' death coming suddenly, after playing golf with
the boys, put the strike away, quite properly, then yogi
berra was the manager, and then the rusty staub trade
was announced, and meanwhile roy campanella had been
put in the hospital and it looked like he was dying too.

it was, again, along with the strike, a sign and a portent,
but we didn't know it then, and it was the real beginning
of exactly the kind of summer the mets were going to
have, with all the injuries, the death of george weiss, the
collapse as it were of the team's world. look, i don't mean
to equate the death of a man with the fun and games,
but if one does posit a universe for a game, then the death
of a team takes the same precedence there that the death
of any human being does in our universe.

i didn't much care for george weiss, abstractly speaking,
because after all, what did i know about him? i knew he
was a hated yankee, who the yankees screwed, and i

knew what bill veeck had to say about him in veeck as in wreck, which was pretty much what i thought i knew already, that he was a cold, calculating, hard man, the kind who had very little to do with my vision of baseball, and who was, for me, thoroughly identified not only with the yankees, but also with the bosses. i was glad the mets had taken him in, because that seemed to me, as with stengel and berra, a needle in the yankees, but i couldn't get rid of the feeling that he was still, at heart, a yankee, not understanding me or national leaguers or national league fans, and indeed we all bitched and moaned those first seven or eight years over what we thought his theories were doing to the mets. we'd look at houston and its trades and its young players and we'd blame it all on george and his damned insistence on box-office draws even if the box-office draws were out of it by now. we knew there were fans here who wanted to see baseball, and national league baseball at that, and who were willing to sweat out young kids, but who were not quite so happy with mediocre "professionals" and who were visibly unhappy over seeing past heroes like hodges and snider and ashburn et al. being used past their greatness. just as we wondered whether casey really was that good for young ballplayers, and used to think how much better an al lopez, with his reputation for teaching, fairness, and careful handling of young players, would be for the club.

but in any event this coming together of deaths, changes, moves all tied into one thing when i started checking it out, and that was the summer of '43, like sinatra said, a very good year. i turned thirteen in february of that year, and we had a party, a catered affair, at the old house on hawthorne avenue in yonkers. it was our last few months in there, since we moved to the coveted, and, 'til then, pretty restricted park hill area in the spring. my father did the whole thing, sort of a farewell party to the old neighborhood including an irisher bartender, maybe the first i'd ever seen outside of the movies, and my father introduced me to him, saying this is the bar mitzvah boy, give him all the ginger ale he wants, which may or may not have had a great deal to do with the drinking that followed for twenty-seven years, and certainly set up a fascination with bartenders and irishers that has lasted to this day despite the efforts of the clancies and hamill and flaherty to dispel all such romantic notions. you have to understand that jews drank in a special way in those days, al koblin being the only one i've seen who still does it lately, and he uses glenfiddich instead of mount vernon, by far the favored brand those days. you tossed the shot back like medicine, because it's good for you, it's a celebration, and goddamnit celebrate. then you throw some water back with the same crisp attack and you've had your drink. and it beats the hell out of sipping j&b and soda, i'll tell you—at least there was some kind of professionalism to it.

so this catered party, a forerunner of the safari bar mitzvahs and the one in israel, was nevertheless an old-fashioned gathering of family and friends, and of course like all such, the family found a way to fuck it up for me, since my oldest brother took this opportunity to announce his engagement, and that was the end of my bar mitzvah prominence. what else are siblings for?

the summer came and the war went on and i was thirteen and a budding baseball player—that may indeed be the summer i caught and hit a ton, but that i'm not certain of—and i remember reading in the *world-telegram,* i thought joe williams or bill roeder, but bill roeder corrected me in a lovely letter and he says it may have been joe williams but was more likely tim cohane, who was covering the dodgers then, that there was a big strong kid from indiana in the brooklyn system. as everybody knows he had two at-bats and no hits that fall when they brought him up and then he went away to the service and when he came back he was gil hodges. well the dodgers went through that season with mickey owen (with no "s," for which i am also indebted to roeder's letter, since everybody does make that mistake) and bobby bragan alternating as catcher and getting a whopping two homeruns between them, and god knows we needed a big strong kid catcher then, but in '47 bruce edwards batted .295 and knocked in eighty runs, and then in '48 campy came up from st. paul with his .325 average, and so hodges became a big strong kid first baseman instead.

and what a white boy like me wouldn't have known about that same summer of '43 was that campy had jumped to the mexican league from the baltimore elite giants, just for the season, as it turned out, but a yankee fan my age would probably have known that there was a kid named berra catching at norfolk in the piedmont league, and, indeed, sometime early that summer, his parents, and only his parents, could possibly know that daniel joseph staub was conceived, to be born april fools' day of '44 (and there's that circle of the year again and the holidays punctuating, over and over, round and round) and he, according to the baseball register, was named rusty almost immediately by a nurse at the new orleans hospital because of his red hair.

see. it really all does come together very neatly. but there has to be the attempt, still, yet and always, to nail it down, make it make sense. those were happier days, i sit here saying now, 1972, because i'm sad that it is 1972 all of a sudden, and gillie is buried, and campy is taking light nourishment, and berra is back managing a club, and staub is packing his gear and moving to the big apple—despite the fact that cavett announced the other night that the squares call it the big apple and the insiders just say the apple and how in hell would he know? —and i'm trying desperately to recall those years and moments of waiting, of growing, of seriously and with all my soul praying for the war to last five years so's i could get in there and show 'em, of buying war stamps, of riding my victory bike that you had to pump even going downhill the thing was so hopeless—again the damned sibling thing, this time it was my middle brother who had racked his bike up so badly at nine that they wouldn't give me mine until i was twelve so i ended up with what schwinn tried to put together out of nonessential materials—and being an air-raid messenger on that very bike, going up and down the blacked-out hills of yonkers the terraced city, like the chamber of commerce used to say. my aunt had the blackout room in the pantry behind the kitchen in her third-floor apartment and we'd sit playing monopoly and all-star baseball, the old spinner-card kind, surrounded by canned goods and bottled water, playing at air raids.

so, the records are there for hodges and berra, campy's must be available in mexico, but staub and i were off on our own. no meaningful records are kept of us that year except in our faulty heads. but this coincidence in time is more meaningful than wendell wilkie's whereabouts or cordell hull's last words. it is a glue of time, the last remaining glue of a universe i just got a taste of, a universe my father foolishly, i see now, believed in, a universe my children will never see, with all its snares and its delusions, its lies, its frosted icing.

we believed, all of us, then, in a world that didn't exist, of good guys and bad guys, of rules you could trust not to change.

in 19 and 43, for example, alvin dark hadn't come up yet, that wouldn't be 'til '46, but he must've already learned the old lies, and would live with them on and on. i'm glad he's not coming to new york, though he was mentioned for the manager's job. i'm sorry i even have to think about it, the old days. the same days, i suppose, but now at least we admit they exist.

i'm trying to explain where i was then, a skinny jewish kid who hadn't learned he could do anything but be, abstractly, smart—i had scared myself half to death jerking off for the first time just that march, and some-times i think i've spent the rest of my life chasing the fear and the glory of that first incredible orgasm, the orgasm you didn't know existed, because joey, my tout, a year older, hadn't described what happened, but only how to get there, only the trip, only the how-to part like the american we all were—and, in that house of yankee-giant-cardinal rooters i had tied my ass to the dodgers, and in the whole city of yonkers i was one of the few who had cried when the ball went past owen in '41, while the yankee fans, the smug bastards, all of them, laughed, and the giant fans angrily accused me, me! of embarras-sing the national league. oh well, i even drank royal crown cola then among all the coke and pepsi people, so, yes doctor, i swam the wrong way even then. how else are poets made!

what the epilogue on this eulogy has to be, then, is rest in peace, gilbert ray hodges, i loved you when i was a kid, and even older, and i argued with you later, second-guess-ing all the moves, but i loved you first; and hang on roy campanella, and berra and staub, be with us and bring us pennants, and oppenheimer, you grow up! it ain't '43, one of your kids will be thirteen in 1984, and what will he hold onto twenty-nine years after that?

my father left me a legacy of lies but he didn't know that. he thought he was handing me a future, and i thank him for trying to. it wasn't his fault he couldn't. and, in fact, i drink all the ginger ale i want to now, the drink of retired heroes. what i want to know is, did joey gallo root for the dodgers too in 1943?

(relative addenda from later in the season: eddie waitkus died september 15, having lived through being shot by ruth steinhagen in a hotel room in chicago in 1949. they had never met. she said later, "i'm sorry eddie had to suffer, but i had to shoot somebody. he reminded me of my father. since i shot eddie, i feel more consoled and relieved than ever before in my life." he made it into a good novel through this accident and also instantly became a member of everybody's all-time all-star bizarre team. if you read the obituaries in the *sporting news* you could go crazy.)

THE RIGHT SEASON

7

who could expect they'd play on a day like today: forty degrees, rain all morning, rain predicted all afternoon, and last year's fiasco for the management to ponder, or on which to ponder. that one started late, had two, as i remember, rain delays, a cold wind whipping through, and ended up a four-and-one-half-inning game. *i* certainly couldn't expect it, so i decided to go shopping. but i put a hedge in, i took the transistor with me so i could check at two o'clock and see if the idiots were indeed playing. given all the factors we've already discussed, i could believe anything. of course i did want for them to play, i wanted the season to begin, but i wanted the sun shining, the wind mild, i wanted baseball weather. there was no way that could be arranged. we might as well have been back in february or march before all the troubles the way the weather was.

at noon i called tom quinn to tell him i wouldn't be watching the knicks on his cable set from now on unless there was no "real" game on, and he didn't understand, and i had to spell it out for him. he's very slow that way

—he doesn't understand about "caring." i care about the knicks, and about basketball, and i care about lots of things, like the announcement of the first new york-phillies game at randall's island next month, but my commitment to baseball is moral.

especially now—when the columnists and the owners have combined to drum up the fan anger at the players. there've been articles predicting booing for the player reps when they're introduced, which will probably happen, now that it's been set up. unfortunately the only antidote seems to be cutting off your nose, etc., by not going to the games at all, which means that you don't put any in the bosses' pockets, but you also don't get any fun out of it. if i can figure out a better way, i'll start a campaign.

so, i took off at one, shopping list and transistor in pocket, and had the list finished, all the shopping done, at two on the button, and was seated comfortably on my stool, ginger ale in hand, at the end of the lion's head bar. i took the transistor out, flicked it on at minimum sound, and cupped it to my ear. koblin started screaming, even though he couldn't hear it. he's an owner after all. schlenk stood behind the bar slicing the limes and laughing and laughing. schlenk is the man who watches gymnastics on slow saturday afternoons. koblin said he wasn't going to allow baseball transistors in his bar. i told him to go fuck himself. i would've said to go *and* fuck himself, but i figured this wasn't a major crisis. koblin claimed he could hear the transistor down at the other end of the bar. this was a patent lie, since i could barely hear the damned thing next to my ear. but i just said it was too bad if he could. i also told him that if this shit was going to continue all season it would make a marvelous thread for the book and it was too bad he was going to have to pay to read about it. i got a hand from the bar for that. i added that it was the quickest i'd ever seen anyone ace themselves out of a free copy. the book hadn't even started being written, after all. this is where koblin told me to go fuck myself. the bar conversation was on its usual level, all was right with the world.

except out at shea, where the opening-day ceremonies were indeed going on. the idiots were going to play and the season was going to start, despite death, economics, and weather. terrific. i had time, it seemed to me, to dash home but i decided it would be only right to stay at the bar and fight it out until staub and fregosi batted. this was magic working again, and the decision, having been made, had to be hewed to. meanwhile koblin kept up sniper fire from a distance, but since the boys were droning on about bill shea's floral tribute, i put the radio away for a while. i smiled at koblin and said that while i knew he wouldn't put the mets on the television i was frankly dismayed to find that he wasn't showing the aba play-off game. he said he had given all the bartenders orders not to allow the aba on his set. i said that first of all it was schlenk's set, he having donated it out of desperation after the bar's set had remained unrepaired and unworking for three months. and i added that it seemed ridiculous since i had personally watched in astonishment while he and schlenk stared at not only schlenk's gymnastic competitions but every sport shown at all, with the possible exception of professional bowling—and especially while they had watched golf. now, golf as a spectator sport *demands* that you sleep. it's not even optional like it is in baseball.

at quarter after two i decided to try again without the hassling so i moved into the back room and sat in a far corner to listen.

in the second inning staub led off with a single, cleon singled, fregosi doubled, and kranepool hit a sacrifice fly, and we were two runs ahead. i went out to the bar, an-

43

nounced to koblin that the trade had paid off, picked up the groceries and went home. the thing about magic is that you have to obey its rules or you blow the whole thing.

having done it right in that sense, when i got home i was treated to a homerun by steady eddie, and then my accountant called, and, mirabile dictu, it turned out i could pay the taxes i owed. so it was a very good day, and despite the strike and the weather the season had started, and we were hitting, and seaver and mcgraw were pitching well.

that night, on the news, they reported that, sure enough, a couple of players' reps around the league had been booed when introduced. i'm sure nothing like that went on at shea. are you?

it's the second day of the season and nathaniel is in action already, having caught the fever. he's discovered baseball cards and has begun trading in earnest and i sense a future for him in the game—which i had worried about, since he is a bit small for his size and seems more the harrelson type of build than anyone else's. he obviously has also inherited from me the abominable habit of shying away from physical contact, not only with people, but with balls as well. but, on the basis of his first trade he's set for general manager some day.

we stocked his team out of lamston's saturday, rather unfairly, i guess, since they had a bin filled with enormous packages of baseball cards with no gum, fifty-four for thirty-nine cents. who could resist? although, as i've said, it seemed unfair to buy so many at one time, and not even have to put up with the terrible bubble gum. still i got four packs, two for him, and one for his friend eric, and one for me, of course. this was to assure a good basic stock so that it would be easier for them to get the principles of trading, i kept saying.

last night we went through his for doubles and came up with about six of them. in fact we had three tommie agees—and two of "tom seaver as a boy," which is a modern-day type i disapprove of highly, because baseball cards are supposed to be baseball cards, not family albums—and also an extra mike kekich, so i figured he might be able to find some action in the building with the eight-year-olds who already seemed to be hung bad enough on either the mets or the yankees to know their names.

then, today he went to play outside and took the cards with him and came back up and reported that he had given michel dobbs one of the agees for a cleon and a broken cap pistol. this indication of a vocation for him was cheering to me, since i was sitting there pretty depressed because we had lost our game.

it was, in fact, a game that provided an exercise in patience and how to stick with it. i was drawn, over and over, to the knicks in their play-off, but managed to control myself and just check their score every half-inning and occasionally during the bottom of the pirate batting order. it is my firm belief that teams hear you when you turn to another game, and that unless you do it carefully and for good reason they get very bugged.

and there was also interference from real life, since the reason nathaniel was outside, the cards being secondary, was that eric's grandparents had given him a two-wheeled bike—a most despicable move, since they didn't warn us, and nathaniel has been going crazy about it—and today eric's grandfather was going to teach him to ride it without the training wheels. i've already told you that i didn't get my two-wheeler 'til much later in life, so i suppose there was a bit of moral disapprobation on my part too about giving five-year-olds toys beyond their capabilities, or else call it jealousy. in any event, after eric learned, then his mother was going to take over and try to teach nathaniel. i felt strongly that i ought to be down there with him during this important step forward, but on the other hand, if i was all uptight about the mets and the knicks, wouldn't that come through and affect him adversely?

this is the same reasoning i have used very successfully to avoid going sailing, horseback riding, and motorcycling with him, and i find i am able to sleep just fine at night.

but all this did mean that i had to keep running to the window between innings and knick scores to see if he was on the bike yet. i felt like the golfer whose partner dropped dead on the fourth hole and, as he said to his wife when she commented that that was terrible, you're damned tooting, it was schlep and drive, schlep and drive, all fourteen holes.

the end result of all this maneuvering and planning and careful attention was that i watched an absolutely dreadful game, one that looked exactly like the mets of 1962. the pitching of gentry and matlack and taylor looked not bad at all, matlack in fact surprising me, striking out sanguillen very nicely, but the hitting, or lack of it, and the mistakes gave me a distinct sense of déjà vu.

they did fold quietly in time to allow me the last five minutes of the knick game, however, which turned out to be a heart-attack sort of five minutes but a win for the knicks. what would have happened if i had watched the knicks and just turned the mets on radio for scores now and then? we would have lost both games. what would have happened if i had gone downstairs with nathaniel and watched him learn to ride? we would have won both. well, it's early in the season and i'm not getting all the vibrations yet, so you win one, you lose one, and that's the way it goes.

monday was an off day. i had to teach my poetry workshop up at city college and i kept thinking how clever i had been to end up teaching on monday so it wouldn't interfere with the games, and i wondered how city would feel if it knew that was the way its distinguished visiting-professor-of-creative-writing's imaginative thought processes went.

before i went up to school, though, third baseball poem came out. i wonder if in fact there can be many poems in the game. i tend to doubt it and i think it has to do with the tightness of the game's universe, the limits so clearly defined. but i presume i'll find out. if my attention is directed this singularly toward baseball, the opinion may be forced to change.

THIRD BASEBALL POEM

on saturday, on
bleecker street a
shirt cardboard
hand-lettered in
the candystore window
: spaldeens.

on sixth avenue, a
headline says
society's laws
force many u.s.
citizens to live
like caged animals

47

there's no sun, the
radio says rain. it
also says they're
playing. for real,
like shirt cardboard
signs. for real.

for real the rain came
sunday night. we were
one and one by then,
cleon three for seven,
i paced the kitchen
caged, an animal, the
rain kept coming down.

on tuesday i gave a reading at jersey city state college, my
second in two years. it was a favorite place even before i
gave the first one simply because of its name—although
i receive information now that the new jersey legislature
is considering changing it to henry hudson state which
would be a drag. as a school it seems no better or no
worse than all the nameless faceless ones around. there
are always a couple of kids who are genuinely interested
and a couple who think they are, and the bunch who
come because they want to impress their teach' or either
bug or impress their friends, and some who wander in
out of sheer boredom, and, also, one always dreams, a
couple of girls with unformed hopes. i really can't attest
to that because i suffer from "outside lock," which strikes
as soon as i leave my limited and admittedly parochial
home base, but the other wandering troubadors are
always snowing me with tales of conquest. something,
however, happens to me west of the hudson and above
fourteenth street.

what i was really hoping to come out of the reading with
was a sweatshirt—for me this time and not for nathaniel
or lem or helen, although i usually get them ones on out-

of-town trips. i desperately wanted one that said simply jersey city state, but of course they didn't have sense enough to market such a marvel and i had to settle for a sleeveless top with blue stripes that had the college tacked on the end. the name was in a horrible script which somehow helped to save the shirt. i suppose it's hip as hell.

my schedule said the mets were due to play at montreal at night but the news that morning had announced the game for two. it was a gorgeous day down here, but who knew whether winter still sat on montreal in mid-april, and so when i thought about it i figured it made sense to have an afternoon game, so i took the trusty transistor just to be safe. i had sort of hoped it *would* be a night game so i could relax with it, since after i finished the reading i was going to have to rush to the bank to put the money for the reading in so i could pay my taxes. this is the perfect picture of a poet in america in 1972: a reading in the outlands, a met game on the tube, and the bank for taxes in between.

i was back in the city by one-thirty and in and out of the bank quickly, and sitting in the head at two, just like on saturday. vic was there and i allowed to him that if he asked al to put the game on he'd do it, assuming it was something vic had to cover (al's reasoning, as everyone else's in that bar, being that journalists work but poets don't have to). vic laughed and asked me if i was chicken and wanted to know why he should do my dirty work for me, but i offered him a dime and he said he'd consider it, since now i was talking business. but he assiduously refrained from letting al hear us. it's terrible to feel like you're in first grade when you're really in a bar.

so i went back to the table by the kitchen and sat down to eat a cheeseburger. of course i turned the radio on again, just like saturday, and al went ripshit again, only this time it wasn't a joke, it turned out, so we went around the bushes a bit. he was screaming that he wasn't allowing any goddamned transistors in his bar and i was screaming again about the goddamned tennis the goddamned golf and goddamn it the only goddamned thing they had never turned on in that goddamned place was the goddamned bowling and i stormed out and home and watched us lose atrociously to that goddamned expo club which we never could beat anyhow.

which is a morality lesson about bars, or cursing, or expansion clubs, but i can't tell which. al called me the next day to apologize for all the screaming and to offer me the use of his office if i really had to follow a game, so hopefully there will be no more boring nonsense for you about the perils of a baseball fan.

we were snowed out in montreal the second game, so i guess it is still winter there. it also means that seaver will go against the cubbies here on friday. hooton is due to pitch for them, and coming off a no-hitter it should be a helluva game. one paper, the *news* i think, said hooton would go thursday night and we'd get jenkins but that ain't a bad match up either, and vic is getting seats, so i called john dobbs and told him we were going so he should spend the five dollars and buy a sketch pad. he was unwilling to invest until he was sure the season would really go.

the weather was good and the seats were gorgeous—for a pitcher's duel. they were up behind the plate, with the field spread out under us. the only problem is that i'm getting old and crotchety and when i go all the way out to shea i want to see mets' hits bouncing off the walls and guys rounding second heading hard for third and all that, and i want to sit behind third base and not worry about how the pitches look. pitching duels are for home viewing, where it's much easier to work magic, surrounded by the charms and amulets.

a game-long strategy conference went on in the row behind us, between some mostly thirtyish, white, fans. to my surprise they were all down on fregosi. of course this is the basic reaction of all met fans to all met trades, seeing how most of them have panned out, but this had interesting racial tones. they were convinced that white ballplayers collapse relatively early and all at once, while black ballplayers play longer and decline more gradually. the guy right behind me said: "he's all washed up. he played ten years and he's through. only the coloreds go on and on." this was all folklore i hadn't heard, since these guys are the same ones who are patiently going to explain to you how black players have no heart.

but, he'd no sooner said it than fregosi took a ground ball, struggled settling himself for the throw and then uncorked one that sailed past boswell's ear into right field and almost set up a run for the cubs. you could see he had lost his rhythm halfway through the move, like when jabbar takes too long setting up his hook and you know he'll miss. for a minute i thought these guys must have some inside information, and then i thought that fregosi just couldn't make the adjustment from short to third, and then i thought about norman marshall cackling about how hank majeski had told him that everybody in the american league knew that fregosi's legs were shot. this was on top of ryan's big first win sunday for california, of course.

but we win the game, and when the runs came for the mets they were on dinky banjo hits, so i got to see a little running. seaver looked fine and pitched strongly with my highly unofficial scorecard showing only three outfield outs and four grounders to seaver and a couple to bos-well, so i guess that would mean they weren't getting around on him. the day stayed sunny but it did start to get chilly—in those seats the sun leaves you around the second or third inning. there was a guy sitting down the way from us, maybe fifty or sixty, not too old, all bundled up in an overcoat. he was up and down for coffee a dozen times, didn't say a word or make a movement that we could tell about the game, just sat and stared, and up and over our feet and back with his container of coffee, which container i notice is getting smaller every year, and he really wanted hot chocolate we found out but the coke butcher told him there wasn't any, and john and i started wondering why he came at all, when coming back to his seat after harrelson's third time on base, he said to me: "well! we got another hit, hunh?" and said it pleasantly, so i guess he did care, after all. when he left in the eighth inning he said, "it's time to go, hunh?" so that gave him bad marks. it is never time to go until the final out.

the other thing that worked out well was the traveling—which i think will determine when we come. the after-noons seem good, we left the house at one and were in the parking lot by one-twenty-five. anyone who doesn't live in new york will have trouble understanding why this is important. but on sunday doubleheaders if you leave at five of noon you get to the ball park at one-five on the button, and if you leave at noon, that five-minute delay means that you get there sometime during the seventh inning. we got hit by the guy selling american flag pins in the parking lot and john tried to ignore him, but i know a lot about protective coloration, so we stopped and each of us bought one. after all, we both have beards.

the big problem at the game (and one that will crop up again) was the cruddy kids. they scream all the wrong

52

things at the wrong times. andy may be right: they don't love the game the way we used to. and i know what i sound like, too. but damnit they don't know anything about the game—they boo when a guy breaks his ass really trying to do something and they yell like hell for pedestrian plays. but in between our bitching and moaning about them, john and i decided the least we could do was keep things up on the home front, so we bought caps for his kids and mine—even an extra small for lemuel. he could take a gi bath in it, but maybe next spring it'll fit. helen went on the defensive at that, claiming he has a very big head. aside from that being part of a very old joke i don't really feel that much of a need to put him out front in *everything*.

i am looking forward to sweeping chicago, but why we should i cannot say. gentry goes next and koosman the day after and one i don't trust and the other i've been lighting candles for for two years and it hasn't been helping much, and the hitting is still dead, despite harrelson's three for four today. this team ain't going to make it on guys like harrelson hitting. oh agee, staub, jones, we got to have you.

there was a sunday a couple of years ago when i walked into the bar late in the afternoon—i can't really remember whether it was fall or spring, but that makes no difference—and the mets had lost two miserably, and the yankees also, and the rangers and knicks and giants and jets had all lost, and i said thank god for bobby fischer. you really can get discouraged in this city, fun city and the center of the world, and can't nobody here do nothing?

but this sunday was a different story, the kind of day you dream of, taking two from the cubbies, coming from behind in both, and the knicks beat the celtics to take the play-off series. with all due modesty i have to let my magic take credit for all three victories, or else clean living and fast, friendly outfielders.

the day started early—earlier for helen and the kids obviously, because it was their cheerful voices fighting over the laundry that woke me at eight. remember that this is a guy who never got up before one on sundays when he was drinking, because there was no sense being awake before the bars were open. now i was awake and there was nothing to do but get up, especially with the laundry waiting. for reasons i don't fully understand, and i doubt can be explained, but having somehow to do with post-partum tristum and/or women's lib i seem to be responsible for getting the laundry done these days. anyone who has seen my normal mode of dressing will realize that this is dreadfully unfair, especially since lem of necessity and helen and nathaniel by choice seem to change their outfits at least eight times a day. i've even managed to come up with a rather interesting throat condition which seems to me to be from an allergy to all the soap dust in the laundry room (it has to be that because it always hits three hours after i do the damned wash), but helen doesn't believe in psychosomatic anguish. so i decided to get out of bed and fight with coffee and the sports pages for a while.

the morning was spent pleasantly enough, even a little time outside with nathaniel while we were waiting to put stuff into the dryers, and then he stayed out to play with eric and lem went in for a nap and helen went down to get the laundry, since i won't fold it, for christ's sake! and it was only eleven, so i had two hours to work out the schedule for the afternoon and get my head working. when lem woke up i decided to take him out for a walk, since the shopping had worked out well last weekend. i mean it seemed to me that god smiled on my being active and helpful even if i didn't. but of course i took the transistor with me for insurance.

i got back to the park at one and sat there a while with lem, hoping he'd be happy outside for a while but he was cranky as hell, so i only got the start of the game in, and that was not good. harrelson led off with a clean single, and lindsey and i and everybody except harrelson knew that's all it was, a clean single, and only god himself knows why harrelson tried to stretch it into a double. he was out by a mile, and i had a sinking feeling which only increased when bozzy followed by tripling and eventually scored. damn it, it obviously was supposed to be a big inning and instead it was only one run. chicago got two as i was bringing lem upstairs—it happening while i was in the elevator and couldn't listen, of course, which is more food for paranoia—and then, helen was napping, so i tried to watch the game while lem played, but again, of course, he stayed cranky. i kept the mets on the tube and checked in on the knicks via radio. which was more bad news—they were trailing. however, i was fortunate in having missed the very beginning, which was when the celtics had jumped to a fourteen-zip lead. i took it as a good sign that now they were staying close.

the mets were doing nothing. however lem was doing something: becoming unbearable, so i decided to get a bottle for him and slap him in his crib for another nap. martyred hero that i was, i concentrated on the fact that helen was getting the good solid nap she'd needed for a week, and nathaniel was happily playing somewhere. or playing happily is more like it, since him i could have put up with. "where are your children tonight?" was that frightening ida lupino title from my childhood. how could they not know i wondered along with all my fellow americans. it's easy, he said at forty-two.

the problem, unstated, all through this monologue is that that business principle about always moving upward until you get to the job you're unsuited to handle is exactly applicable to families: you always have one more child than you should. and i have to say that this last year, since lem was born, is the toughest year we'd had. not to cry, but to offer empathy—whether your mistake was your eighth kid or your first.

anyhow, when the bottle was warm i zonked it to him and he started falling asleep in my arms, so i carried him in and put him in his crib.

i came back to the set and the radio for five more minutes of futility, and then made the big decision of the day: at two-thirty-six eastern standard time, you could look it up, i switched the radio to the mets and turned the television to the knicks.

at precisely 2:37:30 p.m. cleon hit a two-run homer and fregosi followed with a singleton, and the knicks caught up and pulled one point ahead of the celtics. i tried to call flaherty to make sure this was recorded—i wanted people to believe me, but there was no answer. the son of a bitch was at the sheeds' being fed and watching on color, i remembered, so i dialed ziegel instead. he said he believed me.

now that things were under control i felt secure enough to start on the *news* crossword puzzle, having wiped the *times* out during the laundry run. jackson fouled out while i worked on it, but i plowed ahead to get it finished, figuring that i'm committed to that, so i can't stop it and foul things up, and sure enough, as soon as i finish it and lay down the pen, fregosi walks, forcing in another run, and cowens fouls out for boston. which is how magic looks at its very best. you have to go by gut impulse, neither leading nor forcing, following what seems to be pulling you, and understanding that some moves seem wrong at the time or even illogical (doing a crossword puzzle at a time like this?), but once you're committed you're better off hanging in there or you blow any chance of the charm working.

at this point the knicks win and the mets take the first of two, and my mother-in-law calls up announcing a visit and helen wakes up. luckily this all happened between the games, so i got to talk to helen and warn her that company was coming—since she gets mad when i don't mention things like that—and then could settle down to sweat out the rest of the double header.

the second game went very strangely. there were features like dan mcginn retiring eight in a row, the same dan mcginn who had spoiled an opening day for me a season or two ago by coming in in relief and hitting a homer off seaver to beat him. lindsey nelson kept telling me how mcginn had been an all-sports star at notre dame —although it turned out his football was limited to kicking field goals, so i don't quite see how that qualifies— but while all this was going on there was still a game being played and sure enough here beckert drops a pop fly by fregosi and kranepool singles and grote doubles and all of a sudden the score is tied.

my mother-in-law showed up around this point, so i said my hellos and then lay down for a little nap. it was a beautiful baseball nap, too, and i remember things like jones delivers again! but somehow when i woke up we were losing, and then we tied it up, and we went into extra innings.

my mother-in-law had accepted our invitation to stay to dinner, and here we are in the first crucial game of the season. they're all crucial, when the final standings are added up. i know that. but this was the first crucial crucial game. so when i went in to eat i mumbled something about the score, and the book, and the necessity of supporting my wife and children, and like a good american mother-in-law alice immediately understood my need to listen to the game while we had dinner. she even did the dishes when the dinner was over, and helen took care of lem, so i sat in regal splendor for once, with my coffee, listening to the game. i guess this made up for the laundry.

and sure enough, as i took my first bite of cheesecake milner singled, pinchhitting, which was even better. the boys started talking about his great speed, how he could go from first to third on almost any hit—well, of course, not a single to left field—and so harrelson singled off of regan's glove and milner stopped at second. beauchamp eventually pinchhit for kranepool, which led to a great deal of pissing and moaning by me while alice looked at me strangely and helen said not a word. and despite the bitching and my strong feelings, which i can't disguise and therefore can constantly leak over into the magic—the feeling, for example, that we ought to drop him and pick up tommie davis—he singled home the winning run. so much for feelings, and unless ye have faith as in a grain of mustard and etcetera etcetera etcetera.

so now we're four and two and maybe off and running. on to the west coast and a nine-game sweep—or one loss, like i said, for the jetlag.

the problem with the west coast as should be obvious is that they're so far away. this means they live in a different world because of the time change. they wake people up at three in the morning because it's only midnight out there and it's a hell of a party and they miss you, and then, on the other hand you can't ever call *them* because they're at work or off on the lot shooting or some god-damned thing like that. i was reading the other day about somebody's plan to put the whole country on one time zone—basing it in kansas or some such, where the sunrise would be "normal," if there is such a thing, and we'd be an hour and a half early and the west coast an hour and a half late, but at least all the clocks would read eight-five at the same time. and this would mean i could listen to games from san diego at my regular hour instead of hunching over the radio at midnight sweating out the sixth inning. the sixth inning is when i figured we should have the game in hand and i could go to bed. it worked out in two of the three games, actually, and the other we had a good lead in earlier, but then, like they say, there's always the last out waiting, and you feel like you're cheating going to bed in the middle of the game. and of course at base what's bugging me is that up until a year and a half ago i was never in bed 'til four or five in the morning, and a west coast game was just like an afternoon one on that schedule. now, dry, and also having accepted the responsibility of getting nathaniel off to school, i've been getting up at seven, which means that i aim for midnight as the witching hour. once in a while i make it to one and feel like a champ, really showing what i'm made of. the only good thing about the listening now is that it becomes the exact equivalent of listening to a giant-dodger night game in 1945 with the radio very quiet next to the bed so my mother shouldn't hear. only now it's so i don't wake helen or the kids or the give the neighbors what to complain about. oh how the mighty have fallen, he sighed. quietly.

it's also difficult to get your magic to work over all that distance, so i always get twitchy about the western swings—plus the fact that the mets have been notoriously spotty against weak clubs. so that the san diego set worries me all through. not to mention what colbert keeps doing to us. my energy was being divided again with the knicks on top of everything else, but at least they put theirs away quickly, so i could concentrate mainly on the padres. the three-game sweep was a bonus, despite all my predictions and i felt properly thankful for it. los angeles would be a different story. you goddamn betcha.

the problem is that mets fans are by nature and training pessimists (unless they're eleven or under, but even then they learn quick). they have to be. even when we were weak, we blew the easy ones and split the hard ones, and so, now, if it's going good, you have an overwhelming feeling that everything is going to collapse in the next game. and so it was. we took the first one from the dodgers and then suddenly the pitching staff just disappeared and we lost the next two with no pitching and no hitting, which is far far worse than losing with only no one of the above. but things move and groove, you keep saying, and different strokes for different folks you keep saying, and san fran with seaver scheduled was waiting. he's our stopper, you keep saying. but you keep wondering which were the mets, because you got a eight-and-four record, but there are three seaver wins and two wins on dropped fly balls and that makes a three-and-four record for the rest.

it's important to keep distinguishing the real in the simplest conversations: during the class at city i found myself talking about one play in particular in sunday's game. it had just sort of come up with one of the guys, and since i keep telling them everything is grist for the poetry grinder, we followed it along. i was thinking of the play where staub scored on a slide that was absolutely unnecessary, except that cleon was running up his ass. staub had held up on a drive to right center that seemed to me to be obviously going through—fregosi, maybe? —while cleon had kept coming.

but all the while we were talking i was conscious that there were several things working, several levels to the conversation. first of all, for the sake of trust it was important to convince frank that i really did care about baseball, that i wasn't just fucking around. that is, i had to show him that there was a seriousness involved, and that might convince him something about his own work. because he was showing me good poems, but i kept having the feeling they were "assignments" that he was going to do to get out of the way, and therefore might as well do them right. but he writes, even under these circumstances, far too well to be writing to please me. so what i had in the end to get across was that i didn't really care if he ever showed me any more poems as long as he kept writing them at all and writing them good.

but i also had to keep in mind that the rest of the class didn't care about baseball and thought it was ridiculous for a "famous" poet, and their teacher, to boot, to be concerned with trivia like this, with commercialism, with the opiate of the masses. and that, somehow, they had to be convinced of the opposite from frank: they had to learn that while poetry was serious, so was everything else around you, and you couldn't exclude that which intruded itself on you. i.e., not that they had to watch baseball games, but that they had to watch or feel or see something. or there wouldn't be any poems at all to be delighted with.

and then to cap it all off i picked up another layer in me. talking to frank i sounded, for the first time i'd heard it, just like my father—or anybody's father. i mean laying on the word, backing it up with history, all that. he, frank, said that despite the screw-up, the nonnecessity for the slide, it was still the best slide he'd ever seen, and i had to react to that, and wound up telling him about one of robbie's famous slides, going wide past the catcher, the catcher swiping at him and missing and then giving up while everyone in the park, including jackie and the umpire, knew that jackie had equally well missed the plate. jackie, flat on his back, smiling a little, just leaned his arm back and flicked the plate and the umpire signaled safe. and the play happened maybe five seconds after the catcher thought it was over.

everybody has this sort of memory, some glorious moment they saw, some piece of perfection. that's what gives sports its blood, of course. why else would we care? anyone who saw the bannister-landy race, when they hooked up in the canadian meet, the only two under-four-minute milers in the world then, and landy leading, beautifully, running an ideal race, his one look back to check on bannister and bannister, lumbering a bit, forcing himself past landy while landy stared, anyone who saw that remembers his own disbelief and what must've been landy's. well, i said to the guy next to me, in some bar, somewhere, landy may be the best runner, but bannister's obviously a better racer.

or you can just decide, one hot summer day, to stop and watch a bocce game that you don't understand, a game you know nothing about, but stand and watch it, let the sun beat down on you and the old men playing it, and you begin to see the game, and, more important, the minute decisions the game hinges on. i laugh and joke about schlenk watching gymnastics but i have to confess that one quiet sunday afternoon i caught myself watching with him, alone in the bar. sure, i made great comments like what's the paid attendance? but in the end, watching a man do something, anything, better than you believed was possible is a very beautiful thing.

i read up at marist college last week during the san francisco series, and a kid asked me if i agreed with the old chestnut that between genius and madness there was a fine line. i told him that between everything there was a fine line. ask ralph branca.

while i was on that little jaunt, cortland and marist, a three-day trip, we did in the giants, sweeping them too. somehow that led to all the speculation about willie coming to us. which is something nice to speculate about even if only for the memories. anyhow, i missed seeing or hearing the games, except for a little of one as we came into range of whn before the marist reading, but, with my usual luck, i was back here in time for the san diego debacle.

damn it, i walked out on saturday, having a good week's work behind me, with the nets fighting even in their play-offs and seaver with a two-run lead and by the time i got home with the shopping, the damned shopping, seaver had lost, and the nets had been blown out of the arena by twenty-one points. seems like i just can't leave them alone for a goddamned minute.

A BRIEF INTERLUDE

the routine is simple during the week, as simple and un-
varying as when i ran the desk in the printshop and was
a "working" man. then the morning was filled with rituals
and small routines, to get the head started, to get the
heart started. the container of coffee as i arrived, the
petty clerical nonsense, the pencil sharpenings and stock
resupplyings, the warm-up before the phones began, and
the clients started yelling, and the work jammed up on
the floor.

so, now. the same way, but different things: making
breakfast for nathaniel and lem and me, and, after nathaniel's off to school, the paper or a book or staring into
space, letters maybe. and then some work, and, starting at ten-thirty, the game shows: concentration, sale of
the century, hollywood squares, jeopardy, the three w's.
if i'm working they just blare on beside me, without
somehow leaking in. if i'm not, they're the perfect thing
for watching and passing the time. when i was first on
the wagon they saved my life, literally, because they

took up that time i used to start my drinking in, and somehow time is bearable if it is passing in thirty-minute chunks—you get to one o'clock somehow painlessly, much easier than just waiting from ten-thirty on, checking the watch or clock or sun every five minutes. and you pick up the pace of these shows, you know when the commercials will come on, when the stakes get higher, when the final question's due. the half-hours are chopped into little pieces anyone can live through. so i got hooked then, and, i suppose, am paying my respects right now.

but this morning they had bounced them for j. edgar hoover's funeral. not to speak ill of the dead, but for the first time i felt some kinship with the poor souls who protested the apollo broadcasts because they interfered with edge of night or whatever serial it was got bounced for that. i used to watch the serials too, from one to four when i was first wagoning, but as i got able to handle walks outside and visits to the bar for ginger ale they got dropped and there's been no hangover from them. snobbism, of course, because game show-ers have a spurious intellectualism to lay on the soapers, or so they think. the problem none of us will admit is that the audiences, the contestants and the actors and the characters are all the same people.

anyhow, as i was sitting there missing concentration, pete called to tell me about willie, and so concentration would have been missed anyhow. and all i can say is that losing mr. hoover and gaining mr. mays are two of the best reasons for doing without opiates. pete had heard it on wins and called me to see if i had picked it up, or had anything more on it. the story seems to be that the mets and the giants were indeed negotiating the deal last week, while willie sat or sulked out most of the mets series, and it was broken in the long island *press* by jack lang. so wins picked it up, broadcast it, and then, later this morning, the front office issued an official denial which came through the radio around noon.

but, then, jack lang is supposed to be the unofficial leak for the mets to sound things out by (and, i have to interject, that when this appeared in my piece that week, it resulted in the *voice* being passed around the shea press box for the first time in history. and it was, after all, just an assumption). so i don't really know if the deal is going through, but i have to believe it's a strong possibility.

but if willie is, in fact, going to play for the mets, the heart leaps, and koosman's arm and the rain have stopped bugging me, and it could be a terrific day yet.

my first call was to david, who immediately started bitching about snider, hodges, ashburn, boyer, etc. etc. etc., and i had to say, david, it ain't that kind of trade. but david was born in ohio and is a late met convert, which means he didn't start rooting for them until they started, whereas new yorkers seem to have carried the mets in our genes at birth, even if we didn't know it.

patiently i say, david, nobody figures him for every day, nobody figures him to be our "regular" center fielder, you figure maybe eighty games or a couple more, you figure the rest of the time he sits on the bench and the other pitchers worry about him pinchhitting, that's the way you think about him. and you say things like that when boyer came, the hope was he'd make the team a team—well, we got a team now, and even if what it came to was carrying willie, we could do that.

and on top of everything is the fact that willie does come alive here in new york. there was a sunday last year with the giants visiting and flaherty damned near wore out the phone every time willie came up. he demolished us, hitting, stealing bases, making impossible plays. he's got to be happy playing in new york, playing in shea.

and no matter what else, he got to be better than poor jim beauchamp, our present right-handed bench, which is not the strongest right-handed bench in the history of the game, or even in the history of the mets. i don't know what we'd have to give up for willie, but i don't expect it can be much in players, especially since stoneham has to be hurting for money. he's dealing vets away like crazy —dietz and lanier, for instance—and keeps mumbling about his rookies, but at base, the simple fact is that a total of fourteen thousand showed up for the three games with the mets—and seaver pitched one of them—which is a perfect example of west coast loyalty, or as i once named it, california ethics. that was when john fles told me after i had gotten demolished in a fight that i had gotten into to protect him, that he "really could have killed that guy," but didn't because he didn't want to interfere in my fight. but stoneham and o'malley wanted those fans, so they got them. and if it is only money, good ole miz payson got plenty of that.

in fact, a fringe benefit of the deal might be the remodeling of m. donald grant into a human being as far as the mets are concerned, and they might even cheer him when he's introduced every opening day. that would be a refreshing change. not to mention what it might do to the presidential election, since, after all, the pennant guaranteed lindsay's reelection in '69.

but the main thing is what a pleasure it would be just to see willie back in a new york uniform, just to see him at the bat rack. they'll turn away twenty thousand at the ball park the first game he plays for us—and don't think m. donald ain't considering that too. but i forgive him that. mutual benefits you could call it. but that end of it is neither, like they say, here nor there, because what's really being shown is new york class, since nobody can really give a doodly shit what it is that willie does here as long as he's here. sure, i hope he hits .320 and knocks twenty-five out of the park, and i wish he was thirty-two again, but what really counts is his city wants him back here. in los angeles they walked out on the lakers when the knicks started running away with the game; in virginia they cheered and played taps, literally, when johnny roche sprained his ankle in those play-offs, and in milwaukee they laughed like hell when wilt went down hard and hurt. which is why i say you goddamn betcha new york ain't america. you goddamn betcha.

after the glorious suppositions, the twitchy anticipations of last week, this week unfolded like a chapter in some great cosmic novel, with tricky dick starting it off with a whimper and willie ending it with a bang. strangely, the unfolding of the blockade-mining-bombing shenanigans makes me more paranoid than the sheer opening announcement of it because now it begins to look like that great big plot in the sky: he brings us to the brink once more, or as the other willie might have said: once more onto the brink, and the russians don't exactly back down but they certainly don't do anything, and it begins to look more and more like everyone has their angle, like my daddy was wont to say, and it will all work out. i mean the know-it-alls on our side say the blockade won't actually stop any supplies, so that this allows the russians to say they're upset, but they don't need to get rash about their upsetment, and this means that nixon comes out hanging tough to the great american public, but bill buckley is upset on the other hand because he figures the terms have been lightened and this means south vietnam is gone down the drain, sold away, and meanwhile maxwell taylor is explaining jeffersonian democracy by telling us all that if you don't agree with the prez you should still support him because after all he did make a decision and what kind of game would it be if we didn't back him? . . . if you see what i mean. . . .

then the emmy awards come on and the television people show their spine und the weight of the agnew-nixon-justice attacks just like the citizens of boston to an enemy landing on the beaches: they form a hell of a lot of home guards, design and cut the uniforms, and meet and march like crazy, but there don't seem to be anybody on the lines. melvin laird takes advantage of his press conference to inform us that the north vietnamese are marauders, which caused me to look the word up, just for the hell of it, to get at its roots:

to wander in quest of plunder (from the middle french);
    marauder, to play the rogue, beg

is what skeats tells me, and when wins described the rutgers university sit-in that blocked commuter trains in jersey, it used the words "very dangerous protest." dangerous how? dangerous what? what language are all these people speaking?

then the debate on the abortion reform bill repeal: featured were color photos in bloody red and bottled "unborn fetuses" for their side and coathangers for our side. the pictures won, i guess. which, coupled with the parochial-school money debates has to lead a middle-aged cynic to ask: what do those people want, for god's sake? anyhow, rocky vetoed the abortion repeal, and i knew that the phone call to tricky dick had to go something like stay out of my state, you son-of-a-bitch fella.

and in the middle of all this willie did indeed sign with the mets. he sat in uniform with the club friday night, and he won a ball game for them on sunday. anyone who cannot divest this of its bread-and-circuses outer coating and see beneath it to the human beauty should stop now.

in the first inning sunday he walked to start the game, and then scored, and got thunderous applause for every step. out in the field he took a throw and he caught a fly, also to thunderous applause. then, in the fifth inning, with the rain getting heavier and the score tied, he hit a homerun to put the mets ahead, and if the heavens had opened up at that moment to put the game away officially there would have been an awful lot of immediate conversions to all faiths. later on he walked and then was out on what certainly looked like a steal, but on the kiner show he said it was a hit and run—"we did things different on the giants"—and he wasn't stealing at all.

so he went from aging hero to myth to ballplayer in one easy game, which is the best way to do it, and the measure, i would say, of any human being.

i like the last thing best, the ballplayer (given the mythic homerun to set it up), because in the end that's how you play the game day by day, i.e., professionally. the rest of it is magic which is fun, but like st. peter said to jesus: you want to play golf or you want to fuck around?

everybody at shea that day who was of the female persuasion was wearing the straw bonnets the management had given away, it being mother's day, despite the rain. i'm curious as to how well they held up but there have been no reports. these are the same bonnets about which bob murphy, shilling the game the other night before they knew they'd have willie to fill the place, had said: if mom likes to work in the yard or piddle in the garden . . .

which is exactly the right note to sum up this curious and frightening mélange this week turned out to be.

frightening mélange? is such a thing possible? i've caught it from them.

anyhow: mines, brink, bullshit, terror, and a tiny bit of myth not strong enough to survive.

the rule of wei has been waiting for you, in order with you to administer the government. what will you consider the first thing to be done?

what is necessary is to rectify names.

—from the confucian analects

i had started this week by giving the final exam to the poetry workshop up at city college. a poem, any kind, taking off from the sudden and belated appearance of cherry blossoms on the campus. the trees were a gift from eleanor roosevelt, who, as the other old joke goes, i could have saved. knowledge of the gift was presented to me when i tested out a theory of them being useless frivolity while the city goes broke. the dean's secretary informed me about eleanor while she looked at me curiously as if not sure about my seriousness of intent, even if she does call me by an undeserved "professor."

i don't see how i can reasonably expect anybody to write poems about cherry trees even if they get into bomb imagery. and i had, of course, promised them that i would do the assignment myself as usual. i won't. at a reading two weeks ago, even before this whole mess started, i read a whole bunch of anti-war poems, starting almost ten years back—damn it, they will still be fresh twenty years from now, and needed, and willie will be an old man.

everything but the lie dies, yet they accuse us of fucking up the language.

9

SOME ADVENTURES WITH THE GREAT AND THE NEAR GREAT

since childhood i'd wanted to run up a list of perfect things, the perfect murder mystery, the perfect war story, the perfect blues (that was later when i got sophisticated), so i suppose the little flurry in the press box over my calling jack lang the mets' unofficial leak in a piece of mine in the *voice* will have to suffice for my big sports scoop, and i suppose the week or two following the first rumors through willie's settling in with the mets are as close as i'll come to being in on the sports scene.

i must say i'm still convinced that my initial feeling was right, since lang's breaking of the story here in new york did force stoneham off his ass and to the talking table and i'm sure that was the desired effect as far as the mets' front office was concerned. the chances are that willie never would've gotten here if some goose hadn't been given. (somewhere along the way lang asked vic if "leak" meant he had pissed on me, and vic told him that would make a terrific letter to the *voice*, but i guess jack chickened out.)

the important thing about this week or so was the revival of the old art of baseball argument. one guy—a sportswriter—spent hours screaming at me, first putting willie down, and then almost in the same breath telling me how he was a better center fielder than agee. his theory was that the mets, if the deal went through, should put willie in center, agee in right, and make staub a first baseman. all the experts were experting sentimental and rational reasons for the deal to go through. i thought he couldn't hurt the club and he might very well help it.

so the week of rumors and assertions and denials passed, broken only by nixon's announcement of the mining, and finally, willie was signed on the following thursday, and a lot of miz payson's money plus charley williams went to the giants, and don hahn went down to the minors and jim beauchamp gave up his number so willie could wear his old "24." those three names are going to be worth a fortune in trivia arguments ten years from now, so remember them. that is, if there are still bars ten years from now. i'm not so much worried about baseball disappearing, because trivia will remain even if the sport goes. but bars are a different story, what with all those people smoking natural herbs and things.

right after the signing, the next day in fact, i ran into merchant on christopher street, and we were just passing the time of day, like they say, when he mentioned that someone had contacted him about a tv special about willie, and would i like to be on the panel of sportswriters on it? the thing about larry and me is that he thinks poets are some special breed of man and i think sportswriters are, so we're always very deferential about our own end of it, and terribly respectful toward the other's. in other words larry would always downgrade sports talk with me, while i always downgraded the world of poems with him, when in fact we both were always startled to be let in on the other guy's thing. so naturally i started bubbling right away—holy shit, a genuine sportswriter, they want me as a sportswriter!—and in about half an hour we had it all set up, larry and vic and me, and maybe joe if he could make it.

and i was still bubbling when i got home. we were supposed to tape it the next day, saturday. and since friday night's game was supposed to be willie's first appearance in a met uniform i pulled nathaniel away from his dinner to watch the beginning of the game. he was more than a little puzzled by this behavior, since i usually spend most of dinner trying to convince him he really ought to just sit there and try to eat his food, and helen and i were both giggling at me too, but it was a sense of history, corny as that sounds, and i wanted the kid to see this.

we watched for five minutes with a shot of willie in the dugout but no real ceremony and then we went back to dinner. it was probably better that way, just quiet, at least for me. i said something to nathaniel about being able to tell his children about it and i meant it. there were two great moments in my childhood where my father showed me the great world and one was hearing how my uncle had served in the lost battalion in wwi and one was being told about an actual real ruth homerun he had seen. of course that was a different universe, but we do keep hoping.

by the time the taping came around, saturday at five-thirty, we had won two from san francisco and it had been announced that willie would play on sunday. they had decided to do the tape at the head instead of at the studio and so we all met there. i should have been relaxed but instead i was nervous as hell—probably equally compounded of the "sportswriter" tag and the strange fact that the antisepsis of the studio would have acted as a calming agent: i.e., you're on and you know it, whereas trying to get up for a "public appearance" in friendly confines proved difficult. i am always nervous before a reading or any kind of staged thing, and certainly especially so these days without any booze. i once did a thing at channel thirteen in which i thought i was cool as hell until helen pointed out, later, that whenever the camera pulled way back it showed my left hand down by my thigh wriggling and squirming and jumping around, so all the energy was zooming down there obviously. what happened here was that for one of the few times in my life i got frozen-mouthed. the director said later that for the whole first reel my moustache was quivering. we were perched at the bar and i kept sucking on my ginger ale and then, finally, along about the second reel we all started to relax a little and managed to say something at least and then we went home. the show was going to be shown monday night.

so i think i won't be a tv star.

sunday's game, as i said, was all that it was supposed to be, almost as if a script had been written. flaherty went out and he told me when willie's homerun took off he was up screaming get out of here you fuck get out of here, and jeanine whispered to me that joe was crying, literally. we decided there ought to be an official turning-of-the-coat ceremony for him, and for any other old giant fans who wanted to participate, and we did it monday afternoon at the head. joe even wanted to trample his bobby thomson button into the ground but we couldn't allow that—i mean that would have been ex post facto, as the saying goes, and it certainly was okay to have been a giant fan up to but not including sunday, so the button could stay as memorabilia.

monday night the plan was to meet david for dinner, since monday is my city day and i usually eat out, so we planned to watch the broadcast at david's after the meal. helen had a night off, too, over at joellen's, and nathaniel was home with a baby-sitter, so we could all see it separately.

the program started with the three of us sitting around talking, then the camera went out to shea and interviewed fans, then cut back to us, then to willie for some talk, then to shots of willie's great days, and then back to us for the end of the program. so my wife watched the first bit, assumed that was all, and turned it off, and nathaniel was hit by his evening shits in the middle of the program so he missed half of it, and i was the only one who got to see that the show went out with the story about nathaniel missing his dinner to see willie in a mets uniform. oh well.

i stopped over at the head after the show with my pen at the ready to sign autographs, but nobody there had even bothered to watch. which all adds up to something or other about a prophet being without honor, etc., because when i got out to shea for the following thursday's game—and most assuredly shea is not my country—a kid came up to me while i was in the ticket line blurting, "television! television! i saw you on television!" in the best gary cooper manner i allowed him a laconic yup, whereupon he asked me if willie was going to play that day. well, both wins and the *post* had announced that he would, so i figured i was safe in saying that he would. the kid ran screaming back to his friends saying, "he's going to play! he's going to play! the guy from television says he's going to play!" by this time i was at the turnstile and i heard the cop on duty there say something, and say it again, and then i realized he was saying it to me: "long way from the lion's head, ain't you?" whereupon, eddie brennan said to me, "jesus, joel, i was here with flaherty waiting for you for twenty minutes and nobody recognized that fuck," and flaherty smiled. but three hours later when he went into the clubhouse waiting to interview willie, vic introduced him to jack lang, or tried to, saying: "jack, here's somebody i want you to meet"—and lang burst in and said, "oh, joel oppenheimer!" flaherty didn't talk to me for two days. but it was okay, since we won, and, like they say, it was willie's daring base-running what did it. in the first inning he came tear-assing home and knocked the ball out of the catcher's hand, which allowed martinez to score behind him, and that was it. mcandrew won 2–1, mcgraw saved it for him, and this made it 2–0 for john and me. since neither of us could remember having seen the mets win while we were watching prior to this season, we were off to a great start. but we had still seen two tight pitcher's duels, and i was still hungry for the hitting. for that matter so was the team.

and i did get another old-man story: in the seventh inning on my way to the john, i hear this old codger screaming at the stadium cop that there was no doorknob on the inside of the "in" door and by god there ought to be! i guess i hope he wins, because it's a nice fight to spend your time in if you have to have something to fight about. in fact there was a great quantity of gaffers out there, it being old folks' day, but it had sort of wigged eddie and joe and john and me when we first saw the people waiting to get in, because we thought they all had to be old mel ott fans come out to look at willie. about the third inning the scoreboard welcomed them all, so that straightened us out, but then it specifically mentioned the princeton class of '09. then i sort of felt sad that they had to see people like our crew out there on their big day.

this was my first view of the new flaherty in action and i'm happy to say that he and eddie, and tommy sugar who came in late, all acted like they had been yelling for the mets since '62, despite their lack of experience.

then, that night vic and helen and i had dinner with the frisellas and the frisellas came to my poetry reading. there is, in fact, a new breed, and if this doesn't prove it, nothing will. vic had mentioned danny to me a long time ago as one of his favorites as far as talking to went, and had talked about setting up a dinner, and when he mentioned the reading to frisella, he allowed as how he'd like to hear it. so we had a pleasant meal downtown and then went up to the gotham bookshop for the reading. he said he enjoyed it, and i was gassed. i mean, i had watched the mets that afternoon while they did their thing, hadn't i?

and in my defense i have to say that i am much taken with pros, in any field. there is a dedication to doing it right, whether it's a poem or a forkball that it seems to me can make sense to anyone if they're listening.

i expect that i'll have dinner again with them, because we liked them and they liked us, but i think it will be as private citizens from now on.

10

THE END OF THE RIGHT SEASON

my brother-in-law is a very good fan but he knows little about magic and nothing at all about naps. which figures, since he is studying to be a doctor, and they don't consider either to be a part of real life.

i discovered this lack in him on monday, may 29, which was, according to the government and the travel agencies, memorial day. the national league having also accepted it as such we had an afternoon game scheduled with st. louis. in addition, the schools had accepted this abomination, too, which meant that nathaniel was home and raising hell all day, so that when philip and judy called and said they were coming over, i figured it meant good company for me while watching the game and good company for helen while not.

philip and i watched, with a somewhat quiet nathaniel, since his uncle was here and that was company and the score went to 6–3 their favor and we all sort of gave up. not really of course, but there was no sense in sitting and hurting, so philip went into the kitchen with helen and judy, and nathaniel decided to paint in his room, and i was free for my midgame nap. i tilted the set a little toward the couch, carefully adjusted the sound so i could hear it but not so it was intrusive, assured nathaniel, who had popped back out of his room, that nothing new had happened, and stretched out on the couch. it worked. improbably shortly after i closed my eyes boswell hit his first homer of the season with two men on and the score was tied. philip walked in, checked the score, and walked back to the kitchen. i heard him tell helen that i was asleep and had missed it. two minutes later they replayed the homerun, but he thought it was another one and started screaming about me missing the two of them and did helen think he ought to wake me? without opening my eyes and as clearly and loudly as i could i announced that it was a replay and why the fuck did he think i had lain down anyhow if not to get the scored tied?

agee was on, staub was up. i went back to the business of napping and winning the game. i heard philip and nathaniel come in, quietly, as philip warned nathaniel not to bother me. staub reached, mays reached, and agee scored on a wild pitch. we had koosman warm for the last of the ninth so i felt secure finally and settled myself. and promptly fell into a deep, beautifully comforting sleep. i was awakened by a great silence and a deep malaise. the idiot had turned the set off after the last out! any napper knows this is critical. the full nap, with the set droning quietly, is one of god's great gifts to mankind. but how can you convince a third-year medical student of anything relating to body or soul? the consequence was a horrible late afternoon and evening that was only saved by helen producing a fantastic chocolate mousse pie.

when the nap had been broken i had turned on the tail-
end of the yankee game to see if swoboda was playing
(he had started over the weekend and gone four for
eight—and i like to think that that had happened because he had cancelled out on dinner with us, and he
had cancelled out because he was bugged about not playing—but that's an entirely different kind of magic). it
took only one minute to remind me again why i am not
a yankee fan. bill white was talking about some guy's
average and said that some of the players figure if they
get fifteen hits every fifty times at bat they ought to hit
.300. i had to wonder what he thought the rest of the
guys figure, and i even had a kind thought for bob
murphy.

on tuesday night matlack shut out philadelphia. what
will we do if he is in double figures by the all-star break?
he could have sixteen wins by then—or more if tom
terrific lets the other guys go on a four-day schedule.
not that i want tom terrific to sit down. but it would be
interesting to see if there's any way two guys, say, could
pitch every fourth day, tom every fifth, and two more
bounce in and out to make up the difference. i'll work
it out—and it's possible that that's how it worked with
the preacher and with whitey ford.

in any event matlack really looks okay, capra is spotty
but shows signs, and koosman has looked good the last
two times in relief. yogi is quoted as saying one more
good go and he starts, and finally, while i still refuse
to believe in mcandrew, he may do it to me yet. he looked
terrific the last time out against st. louis, and he wasn't
that bad at all in the montreal game.

in fact, for the end of may, things look very rosy. we
shall see what we shall see, of course, but it is a fact
that the world at large—i.e., all those who do not under-

stand my fascination with the game, with the team, and with the season—think of the mets as twenty-four guys limping or being hauled along behind tom terrific and it would be nice to have that impression corrected. just as it's nice to see agee, harrelson, and grote doing something as well as staub, mays, and fregosi. and when cleon starts hitting it's going to be even nicer. as it is, i haven't had the heart to tell nathaniel that cleon is slumping.

the one thing we americans can't seem to accept is finesse, and we're always looking for the leader, the strong man, the guy on the white horse, even though those are the guys we (at least the white european segment of the population) left home to get away from.

for example, nixon's astonishing rise in popularity as attested by the ubiquitous polls right after the mining speech. it was direct action, a lot of steam on the ball, blow it right past them, baby.

on friday night, on the other hand, phil niekro got booed at shea stadium on his way to a three-hit win for atlanta, and it wasn't a met defeat they were upset about, it was niekro's knuckleball, a pitch which has always seemed vaguely unamerican to fans. and on saturday tom terrific just couldn't stop bitching about ralph garr's three-for-three, which in tom's inimitable term "didn't make ninety feet between them."

this was new york, where, like they say, excellence is appreciated—and it usually is, too, except when it smacks somehow of conniving instead of strength, brains instead of brawn.

the boos came mainly whenever niekro threw his floater, a big nothing rising high and dropping around the plate, and they were biggest the one time it dipped over for a perfect strike. they call this kind of pitching shit. even the name notes the utter contempt in which it's held. i've thrown a floater, and a lot of other junk pitches, but it's true that the floater bugs even the umpire. nobody notices that hardly anyone ever hits it. i know, i know, that once rip sewell tried to throw one past ted williams in an all-star game, and williams blasted it, but williams was the greatest, and nobody else much that season hit it big that i recall. sewell won 143 games and lost 97 for a pittsburgh team that finished as high as second only once in his ten years, and the rest of the time was fourth or worse, so he can't have been that bad a pitcher. he called the ball an "ephus," which is enough to remember him for.

you see, it's like a betrayal, that a pitcher should throw a pitch that by its very nothingness is hard to hit. a rex barney heaving a bullet past you is a hero, even if he hardly ever throws a strike, because that's strength, man, and power. now don't get me wrong, because i get suckered by that mystique too, and indeed, one early spring day in the fifties went out to the ball park in asheville, north carolina, to see what was to be barney's last appearance in a dodger uniform, although we didn't know it then. the brooks were playing their asheville farm on the way up to brooklyn, and they'd announced that barney would pitch in rotation until he pitched himself on or off the club. it was beautiful. he threw his smoke and threw his smoke and then he threw his smoke ten feet over the catcher's head, and then he gave up a triple and a double and then he put his glove down on the mound and pulled himself and walked to the bench and out of the game.

the point is that the junk pitcher exists by brains alone, fooling you by where the ball is, or might be, or ought to be, and by changing speeds from slower to slowest, and making the ball dip and break or not until you're crazy. you've also got to supply all the power—you can't just meet the ball and watch it sail. this is, of course, what causes all the hostility, since everyone is the same: if they get beat they want to get beat by a haymaker, not nibbled to death, or falling stumbling over their own feet.

kiner was really upset, having been a slugger, and went on and on about knuckleballers until i expected to hear that he had lobbied vinegar bend mizell into having federal legislation introduced banning them. he was so shook that he erred about washington's famous staff in the forties which at one point had four (wolff, niggeling, leonard, and heffner), not three knuckleball starters—you could look it up. it may in fact be that staff that started me on my deviant way, since my american-leaguer team in those days was the senators.

but the simple fact is that all the rules of the game call for is that the pitcher throw the ball in such a way that it pass through the strike zone and is hard to hit, and it don't nowhere in all the fine print say anything about that ball having to be a high hard one or a fast-breaking curve.

the same basic truth holds for garr's three hits, since his job is to get on base safely, and the fact that he beat out two bunts and an infield grounder, and that, in fact, he did the same thing consistently all last season, ought to be to his credit, as much at least as kiner hitting homeruns year after year. but we really can't accept this kind of thinking, and we underrated clemente next to mays or aaron because he hit a lot fewer homeruns —and indeed, in san francisco the fans liked willie himself less than cepeda and mccovey for exactly the same reason. we like goliath, the big lug, is the simple fact;

deep in our souls we really despise david, we think he was cheating somehow.

in the same fashion the landy-bannister race i mentioned earlier found everybody really admiring landy and somehow sneering a little at bannister, who after all, didn't even finish properly. he had given so much to win he fell down after finishing, whereas landy had the grace and style to run his extra lap out.

i'm sure there's something pertinent here in regard to the candidates and the issues and the new theories of populism in all this, but i haven't got the slightest idea what it might be. maybe, in the end, it all comes back to trust. maybe we just don't trust, can't believe in, the man who is so transparent we see what he's throwing, what he's doing, and yet we still can't hit it, or the hitter who dumps one that should be handled, it looks like, but it can't be; maybe we can only buy the pitch that can't be seen, the hit that can't be touched.

it would certainly be a simpler universe that way, and yet, and yet. when we were playing those sunday games ten years ago emilio cruz spent a whole summer screaming at me and my shit, but in one hundred at-bats he got ninety-eight pops to second, a grounder to short, and a scratch single through the hole, so who won that one, and who's better, if you're counting?

it's also significant to me that the three met hits were all gotten by john milner, who's really too young and inexperienced to know that niekro's unamerican. he just went up and tried to hit the pitches.

there'd be no key to the city presented if hoyt wilhelm signed with the mets, but i'd love to see him out there, an old man with a knuckleball and a lot of wins and a lot of saves and a low era and also, a large set of pitching brains. if he lost, it'd be a goddamned banjo hitter beat him, scratching for a hit, screwing around on the bases, sliding home under the tag. mr. kiner, mr. seaver, mr. amurrican, that also happens to be baseball. and, fortunately for all of us, it's life too.

11

INTERLUDE

we were out having lunch with the mexican novelist and he said that at least in mexico you knew which four months it was going to rain and that, furthermore, when it did rain it happened between, and always between, the hours of two and five. i said that was very nice. i said that the atlantic seaboard from philly to boston was notorious for its changeable weather. i said we have a saying here that if you don't like the weather, just wait five minutes and it'll change. i did not give mark twain credit for this remark. so much for wit, deep thought, and honor among writers.

in any event i can't explain why it's been raining for two weeks. on the way to lunch the mexican novelist strode forward manfully, and bareheaded. i was hunched under my new umbrella. novelists like to walk in the rain, it gives them new material or allows them to think or something. poets, on the other hand, take forty-two or so years to break down and buy an umbrella. they do not like new material because they are always hopelessly hung up trying to figure out what the old stuff means.

the one thing that is old material and also doubtless at this point is that tempers have frayed from this recent siege of weather. i wish i could report that we are all responding valiantly as we did during the power blackout. instead we are all drowning, the incidence of marital fights has risen sharply, people either snap or keep sullenly quiet. my building had just started a rent strike when the rains began, and the other day one of our pickets showed up with a sign literally accusing the landlord of starting the rain. even the mice have gone crazy.

as agnes bore in on us i caught three of them in a half-hour, and i'm convinced they just decided to end it all. the theory got further support when my neighbor norman yelled at me for being chintzy with them by serving a very small portion of cheese. norman helps me empty the traps, since when alone i just throw the whole thing, trap and mouse, away, whereas he is very saving and throws the mouse away, sterilizes the trap, and sets the same one out again. norman felt very strongly that the mice ought at least to have a chance at a hearty last meal but i was down to canadian cheddar and was not about to be prodigal with it. what do those mice want anyway?

and even dear old reliable tex antoine, weathercaster supreme, is cracking under the strain. he flipped the other night and roared into the camera that "you" should stop demonstrating your "ignorance" to "your children." this, i'm sure, was an answer to another one of us poor bastards who was asking him about the atomic bomb again. i don't know why the suggestion that the atomic bomb might have influenced the weather enrages him, since everybody knows it's true, but it always does. except that usually he's cool and snide with his putdown. he may be getting angrier now because he suspects we know something he doesn't. in any event it was a very rainy day in new hampshire so many years ago when mrs. milsner came running out of the camp wah-kee-nah (where i played right field while my father watched, remember?) office to yell that we had dropped the automatic bomb, we had dropped the automatic bomb!

i found out twenty seconds later that the word was atomic, since she had the *times* right there in her hand, but the initial impression was so strong, that's how i still think of it.

tex antoine, however, doesn't like inferences that the weather is controlled by anything but him, and since the *new york magazine* survey of selected new york salaries showed that tex is twenty-two times more valuable to society than me, i suppose i ought to believe him, or at least lay off.

so, the rain madness goes on and on. there are supplemental annoyances like rain-outs of games, so you can't even immure yourself securely before the set—there is that one advantage of basketball and hockey and football, i guess, that you know they're going to play the game no matter what the weather is—but then, in the longer view, it is giving rusty and cleon and willie and all time to heal their wounds.

i, myself, am very upset about these injuries because they seem strangely reminiscent of the "original" mets. rusty and boswell hurt themselves swinging at a pitch, tommie and willie hurt themselves trying to catch balls, and cleon got it trying to make a put-out at first base. i mean, these are all things you're supposed to be able to do without getting hurt if you're a baseball player.

ever since the big winning streak in may, eleven in a row, disaster has followed the team, and in fact we've been playing under .500. i think i have to blame it all on eli wilentz—i was in his book store near the end of the streak and he told me, "it's no fun to watch any more. they keep getting five runs in the first"—and eli's was a metsy wail if ever i heard one, and one guaranteed to get to the ear of heaven. it did.

perhaps god is striking out at hubris again—i mean with a twenty-one-and-seven record for may, you begin to think funny things way too early.

and, aside from the hubris problem is the fact that the magic is all screwed up again, since midsummer night came and went, and who could tell? that's the night you're supposed to remember your dreams so you can see the year ahead, and there was no sun all day before it, and none the next day after it, and, in fact, the longest day in the year ended up having less light in it than the shortest.

the conventions keep looming ahead. suppose it's still raining then and keeps raining straight through? despite the fact that only the goyim are silly enough to want to go to miami beach in the summer, it does not bode well.

after the act, and after the season, it's sad to see my initial reaction to the injuries. but who knew? not even the doctors knew about staub.

12

july 4th

the old man had none of the "dignity of age," which is to say he was scruffy, paunchy, pasty, and just old. he stood on bleecker street across from abingdon square park and he was bouncing a spaldeen off the apartment-house wall. he wasn't using the sidewalk, just through the air to the wall and back to him, and he was using his fist, not an open palm. he kept the ball going for about twenty bounces and then, finally, he missed and it hit the ground. then he looked around guiltily, as if he realized how he might look, an old man playing bounceball, so when he picked it up he tossed it a little in his hand, as if he were just standing there, maybe waiting for his grandson.

but while it had been going there had been a rhythm to him like soccer players show when they're jinking around, keeping the ball in the air, head, elbow, foot, just keeping loose. and with his fist balled as if for punchball. that's hard.

he was too old to be keeping loose for anything at all and that shamed me. while he had been working out, a kid stopped by the light had stood there watching. amazing. old man of the sea?

because the conquest is always of time and the body and not taking shit from either one.

the second game against san diego listed the following lineup:

1b: mays, who, still suffering from a pulled leg muscle, had nevertheless played the first game in centerfield.
2b: garrett, who in the first inning, on practically the first play, was hit in a collision at the bag, thus reinjuring his bad knee. he was replaced by boswell, who had been sitting on the bench because of a spike wound received in montreal two days earlier.
ss: harrelson, who was healthy but should, at this point in the season, have been getting occasional rests, like the second game of doubleheaders. his batting average is going down and down, and he needs a couple of days off.
3b: fregosi, who had been hit on the wrist in batting practice a few days earlier and was still feeling it, but was playing third so garrett could play second instead of boswell.
rf: milner, who also, like mays, still had a leg pull to worry about. he was in right field despite the winter book, which listed his major weakness as his fielding, but he was still stronger there than . . .
lf: beauchamp, who is listed as a first baseman-outfielder but is actually and mostly has been over a ten-year career only a pinchhitter.
cf: martinez, who is the one sure bonus of the season so far with the exception of matlack. what a hell of a way to find out about him, though. we knew he played the whole infield, and now he started in right field in the first game, has played left as well, and was listed as the emergency catcher when the season began.

strangely enough the only healthy position was catcher, both grote and dyer holding up, although grote had had to sit down a few weeks before, which was when dyer went wild for two weeks. (not publicly announced at this point was the arm injury that was to incapacitate grote for the balance of the season except for occasional appearances. the mets for some reason—i like to think it was a realization that no one could believe or handle another major injury, but that's me being romantic again, since it obviously had to do with trade values—kept the story under wraps until a week or so before the season ended.)

the mets lost. it was a tough game, but it was a loss. seaver had thrown a one-hitter in the first game and of course that got all the ink, but this was the game that said it all about the club. we are hurt bad. the record at this point is forty-three wins and twenty-seven losses, but that's because of that twenty-one and seven may. june was twelve and fifteen, july is two and two, so far.

on the bench but not available were jones, staub, and agee with their old injuries and marshall with an upset stomach, not to be ordinary. on the bench, and available, was a very healthy eddie kranepool. why aren't they playing him? this is no time for lefty-righty games, or whatever. he certainly could have started in the outfield, and he should at this point be playing every day, damn it.

i look at the schedule and i see a hope, but it's a fan's blind hope, of course. it runs like this: put jones and staub on the injured list, see if sudakis is healthy and can do anything, pick up tommie davis if he's still available (i think he may be—and they should have gotten him as soon as oakland let him go. he hit for them last year, he could do something for us now the way we're hurting. again, he has to be better than beauchamp). if jones and staub can be back by the all-star break, and if we can stay playing around .500 ball 'til then, and the pitching ought to be able to do that for us, then we still have a shot at it.

but this is all, as i know, desperation. the simple fact is that when you sit people like staub and jones and agee down because they're hurt it hurts everybody else too. back at the beginning when mays or milner played they had a pride thing, i.e., willie was eager to show he wasn't gone yet, and milner was eager to show he belonged right now. but when they become the starting outfield day after day it becomes a burden, too much for willie's legs, maybe too much too soon for milner's head. there's also the point that there's nobody in the batting order to scare a pitcher now, at least consistently, which means the stronger guys can be pitched around, and the weaker guys don't get the extra hits they would with the other guys in. and then the pressure falls on the pitchers, and how much can they do with no one scoring runs for them? i'm afraid it's a very old story. fregosi is hurt because he can't come back slowly, milner won't make rookie of the year being played this way, boz and garrett are having to play too much at the wrong times, and martinez is being pushed around like a yo-yo and we ain't going to win a pennant this year.

and, it is equally obvious, the other we, here at home, ain't getting a vacation. after justifying my not going to spring training by looking forward to a long weekend in montreal for that series, we didn't get there either. no way to take care of the kids, which is another old story for young parents. my mother-in-law is in israel, god bless her, and much as i love her, i sure wish she was home with nathaniel and lem. she asked helen if she couldn't do it for us later in the summer and helen passed the question to me. i said, sure helen, where would you like to go, philly or st. louis or pittsburgh or chicago? and that was the end of that discussion. there are times when i'm glad i'm not a sportswriter.

and it's not that we're antiamerican or anything but i keep remembering the one time we'd been in montreal. late one night in a college-type hangout i asked for a sandwich. the waiter allowed as how they had ham and cheese sandwiches but that was all. i said okay. he re-appeared with two small loaves of fresh french bread, slabs of country ham, and a huge chunk of just-ripe brie. now that's a ham and cheese sandwich. and the next day, in a small restaurant when helen ordered the cold boiled lobster she got, for christ's sake, home-made may-onnaise with it. that's, like they say, living. i used to set the hellman's ads and unless i'm mistaken west of the mississippi it's called best foods.

and so to bed after another fourth. the old line is that this is the determining point. and we are determined down-ward, methinks. all one can do is hope.

the democratic convention started last night. in the eighth inning with the mets down 5–4 (the result of mcgraw, of all people, giving up two runs in the top of the eighth) garrett led off with his second hit. this was a novelty of and by itself. i can't be sure because i haven't checked back, but i believe this was his first two-hit game all season. kranepool came up in what they call an obvious bunt situation. which is what he did, to the pitcher, on the ground. they played to second and on to first for the giants' fourth double play of the game. which is exactly the way it's been for four weeks or more.

happily i wasn't watching, only listening, because of the convention. today will be an even worse problem. fischer and spassky are scheduled at one, there's a meeting here in the building of the rent-strikers at seven, and at eight there's the game and the convention—with the platform fight scheduled for tonight. but if last night is any preview, i can probably watch the whole game and then tune in the convention and still see all the action.

to cap it all, lem woke up at five-thirty this morning. he has no sense of priorities. but, i must admit, he is shaping up. he used to wake up at five-thirty all the time, and now it's seldom enough that we are shook by it when it happens. which is to say we used to be shook all the time.

sometimes it works out all right, even if not often enough. they brought dave schneck up from memphis in the texas league to play the outfield, finally. the problem was not only with our guys being hurt, but that tidewater doesn't seem to have any outfielders either, the strengths there, according to the weekly reports in the sporting news, being at first and short.

i mean i suppose we could bring don hahn back up, if you just want a body which happens to be named outfielder. i have to love hahn, though, since he went on his holdout this spring. i mean what can a guy who's been hired as agee's caddie hold out for?

anyhow, schneck comes up and wins friday night's game with a homerun. for our club that's fantastic. it's great for any club, but the mets have a history of bringing guys up who looked all right down there and it takes three seasons before they turn into anything. cleon was like that, as i remember—yes, i just looked it up: in '63 he hit .360 at auburn and .305 at raleigh and .133 in six games with the mets; in '64 he stayed in buffalo; in '65 he hit .269 at buffalo and .149 in thirty games for the mets. so, no big dreams—big hopes, yes—but schneck did lose two years in the army, and every year he's played he's slugged over .500. last year at visalia it was .688 with twenty-six homers in seventy games and that's certainly legitimate. this year in spring training he hit the shit out of the ball but, properly, they sent him back down for seasoning, like they say.

the mets have never had the luxury of, or else have never allowed themselves the luxury of, letting kids come into their own on their own. harrelson was perhaps the only exception—they got mcmillan back in '64 specifically so bud could work alongside him, and that paid off. but the rest of the time it's always been a desperation situation and the choice is throwing somebody in before they're really ready, or trading them for an "established" player. like as no met fan is liable to forget for many many years, amos otis to kansas city for the one and only joe foy. or stanton going as the throw-in in the ryan-fregosi deal. except that this year when the season started we thought we had no problems in the outfield. and we shouldn't have had. we started with jones, agee, and singleton, backed by jorgenson, marshall, milner, and hahn, and while not the greatest ever, it was certainly okay. then the trades and the deals, and for that glorious month or so it was cleon and tommie and rusty and willie and milner, with marshall's bat hanging around, and that may have been the best outfield, on paper at least, in the whole national league.

but the rookies—like i've said, playing in that position, fifth man in that outfield, you get bounced in and played once in a while until you get hot and then you go for a while, and then you come out for a while, and the pressure's off except the good pressure of trying to make your own chance. but when the club is desperate and you have to say to a milner it's you every day no matter what, and you have to pull a schneck up from double a and say you got to save the club, then it's a different story, i think.

99

but we're in san diego, trying to recover from the last awful couple of weeks—or month more like, and we're going against arlin, who hadn't given us an earned run in twenty-two innings, and seaver started off just exactly the way he's been doing it for that month, giving up two runs in the first—although this time not his fault, since it was a botched double-play ball that let colbert come up with a man on, instead of him leading off in the second inning, and of course the ball went out for his fifth homerun and twelfth rbi against us. if you project those figures against the whole league for the whole season he would have 81 homeruns and 175 rbis, which, i should think, might call for a raise for him next year.

but anyhow schneck came up his third time with a man on base and hit one out himself, so we ended up with three runs on two hits, which is our best mileage of the season, and a refreshing change from what seems to me our usual one run on three hits. schneck now has a slugging percentage of 1.000. and arlin? arlin must have an ulcer, to lose like that. it's a good thing roger craig is the pitching coach at san diego, so the guys know that there's someone around who understands about getting beat when you throw two-hitters and such.

most important, given the way things have been going, schneck didn't get hurt. he did make an error, but the papers say today that it was a bad call on him, that he did bobble the ball a little, but the guy had the extra base anyhow. and to add to the sunshine, staub took batting practice, and at least he could hold the bat. progress is progress, but, dear god, we got to get healthy soon.

meanwhile it's hot as hell here in new york and the outfield is nice and dry. why do the yankees get sunshine while we get swamps? is there some sort of chicanery in this? doesn't god know that ruth and dimaggio and mantle are long gone? which thoughts led into just another long, hot, damp night, summer in the city.

and through a long, hot, damp day, so miserable all you feel you might do is make love, tried twice but nathaniel came home the first time and lem woke up the second, so i sit listening late at night to stories of tijuana just across the border in between pitches in san diego. perhaps we can sneak one in, in the dark of night? nathaniel and lem are veritable leron lees when it comes to breaking up no-hitters, or, a better image, perfect games. well wotthehell wotthehell, archy used to say or was it mehitabel? don marquis being, as is obvious, an early early influence. toujours gai, kid, toujours gai.

in this here game, the one on the radio, schneck only gets an infield hit but milner gets three for five, one of the outs being a long long drive all the way to the wall and caught against it, and the paper says harrelson fucked up standing around watching it go instead of tagging up and moving down, which would have meant a run since schneck's bingle followed milner's clout right on its tail. which brings me to that subject again, which always happens when it's hot and damp like this. homeopathy. or else wonder why a forty-two year old poet with a beautiful young wife and two beautiful young children watches baseball games night after night after night. because the kids are always always waking up or coming in, it says here in every heart.

at what age, please, do they go out to play the whole day long? and sleep the whole night through?

gentry lasted as usual until the seventh but they were driving long balls all over him and mcgraw came in. now what is this? do we need it? third time in a row he's not sharp, again colbert at bat, out it goes again—but this

101

time nobody's on base, and the tug gets out of the eighth on a tap to the mound by gaston. by the grace of god san diego had no bench to put up in the ninth and we win. it was sudakis' single way back in the first, with two runs scoring, that held up.

as of this moment this is next year's roster:

if:		of:	
	harrelson		jones
	fregosi		agee
	martinez		staub
	boswell		mays
	garrett		milner
lb:	kranepool		schneck
	sudakis (3b–c)	c:	grote
	dyer		

which looks okay if everyone is healthy. such are the uses of adversity.

except I can't figure out any way to use a new york heat spell.

hot sunday afternoons are no better, in fact, than hot sunday mornings, which are no better than hot saturdays, etc. the game was on at four, though, which allowed me three hours uninterruptedly with bobby fischer. i took only one and a half of them though, just to get out of the house, do something. I walked over to the head, picked up a rye bread for dinner—we're going to sue and gordon's and i only had a slight argument with helen about that starting too early but finally got her to convince sue we shouldn't start before seven.

which is just about when the mets lost the game, having given up four runs in the seventh inning on bad throws by koosman and frisella. lord, do you need to do this? i mean, fielding errors by the pitchers? two in one inning? i can't believe it. how long, oh lord, how long? the final score was 7–3.

this morning i had a little game with nathaniel's friend joshua. the two of them plus eric showed up around ten-thirty. since nathaniel and eric are both five and joshua is seven, i don't understand the relationship, but nevertheless all summer long they've been running together. joshua had his damned yankee cap on, and he's already gotten to nathaniel insidiously, so that on at least two occasions nathaniel has told me with great emotion, dad, i really like the yankees. so i told josh he wasn't allowed to wear a yankee cap in my house. he stood there stunned. i told him i just couldn't allow it, and that he'd have to take it off when he comes in, that he could stuff it in his pocket if he wanted, but that was it. why, he asked? because this is a met house, i said. this is cruel, but so is life. i mean i can't put up with the heat and traitors at the same time. besides, kids should take off any hat when they come into the house, right? saves the moral fiber of the country, right? he folded it up and put it away.

and while we're on young fellers, schneck kept it up yesterday, despite the loss, with a single, double, and another homerun. if we can go two and one against both los angeles and san francisco we are .500 for the month going into the all-star break, and i still have delusions that we have got a shot. there are three with pittsburgh right after the break, and i'm hoping that the outfield will be back healthy by then, everybody, and that in the meantime the rest of the squad can use the break for nursing the more minor injuries. a healthy club is a happy club! we might could even run then, like the man says.

but in the meantime what i have to look at is a seven-and-five season record against san diego which is disgraceful—even considering what colbert and arlin have done to us. i mean, first of all, that we blew a couple of them—the fourteen-inning game down the drain, and yesterday's seventh inning—and secondly that we keep doing it with the other expansion clubs. our record against houston, san diego, even montreal is and always has been shameful. let cincinnati lose to the new clubs, they're after all the oldest club in baseball.

my accountant was on the phone this morning trying to figure out why the gummint is charging me $16.03 for paying my taxes in full and on time, and his wife says to me that she loves the stuff i'm writing for the *voice*, except for when i talk about baseball. rose, i say, that's what the hell i need an accountant for, the baseball stuff. that's where the money is going to roll in from. i don't think she believed me. but at least she's in better shape than one of my neighbors here in the building. she read a dreadfully piggy piece by me suggesting all sorts of terrible things and she told another friend that she "knew joel was interested in baseball but she didn't think he cared about sex." so much for image.

the visit from the ex-wife had been expected ever since primary time back in june when she had informed me of her selection as a mcgovern delegate from new mexico. i looked forward to it, which i suppose is a rarity these days, but i not only once loved her and still, like they say, respect her, but indeed i like her. she's a good woman. but naturally i was nervous. i mean, i do have a wife thirteen years younger than me, and a new family, practically fresh from the crate, in fact. how helen was feeling about the visit was hard to tell. the first year we were married if i introduced her to someone as my wife she looked over her shoulder to see this mythical creature she was sure had appeared behind her. but recently she seems to believe she is indeed mrs. oppenheimer. after the last couple of years she'd better believe it, in fact.

the plan was for cissie to move slowly up the east coast, visiting her mother and her brothers and then stopping to see some old friends in jersey, and on to the city for one night before taking off for new mexico again. she'd last been here in 1960.

just to keep things even she came two hours later than contracted for, so the kids were asleep. she climbed the ladder to look at nathaniel in his loft bed, his face covered by his "feeling blanket" despite the heat, so that helen had to go up and pull it off to show what he looked like. helen said later his soul was gone, his face thin and drawn inanimate. then, shoeless so she wouldn't wake him, the ex-wife tiptoed in to look at lem.

we spent one hour and a half talking, mostly, of course, about the kids, about these two and about nick and dan way out there in the west. what else should we discuss after all this time? i spent nine years with her when we were very young, and all i could remember, visually, was one glimpse of bare breast the night we slept over at her uncle's house twenty-one or so years ago. even her legs, which i had thought i would remember perfectly, looked different. but i had a returning vision of what she had seemed to me the first time i saw her. that other world. the beautiful blonde shikse my mother always warned me about. unfortunately that wasn't what the problem turned out to be. but the problem, or problems, were long gone, and we sat relaxed, helen too, and talked. i had worried, sure, but i was glad she came by.

but what it did do was blow the los angeles series. i lost the first six innings of the opener by the late visit and that started it all off wrong. i listened to an inning and a half before i went to bed with the score tied 1–1. at eight-fifteen in the morning, i caught the details of the end of it on wins. we had lost in the tenth on frank robinson's homerun. there's the whole history of a broken marriage right there.

on the other hand helen and i have quite often worked sexual magic during games. how else do you think we won the series in '69? that pun is not intended. for something as important as the world series we would certainly use only straight-on, nonperverted magic. the play-off series was a different matter.

what helen did do this morning was to say it's terrible to have to think of waiting 'til next year, isn't it. she's right. it's terrible, and i guess we have to.

because to do it this year the following improbabilities must all come to pass: staub has to come back; we have to kick the shit out of philly, montreal, and chicago, while we hold pittsburgh and st. louis even in the east; and take three from san francisco, hold atlanta and cincy, and do what we've never done to houston, cream them, in the west. i think, at this point, we can't do it. but one hopes.

the team seems stronger than at the start of the season, as i keep telling myself, and have mentioned in these pages. but it's true, damn it. staub and agee are still problems, but for the rest cleon is playing again and should now start doing what he was supposed to be doing all season long, which means that willie, who's already more than paid off on his end of the deal, should now get a little more of the rest he must need. milner is fine and there's no question about that now, while schneck has started hot and until proven otherwise we're in luck there. marshall has been doing what he's paid for, filling in and pinchhitting. harrelson's lost his bat this season, it seems like. probably from the lack of rest earlier on, but we need him in the field and he's been fine there. fregosi, of course, turns out not to be the final solution, but he's the best we've had, except for ed charles' magic season. martinez i've raved about already, and with boswell and garrett we have to fall back on the old baseball chestnut, that they will reach their averages. which, after this terrible start, should mean a hell of a lot of hitting from both of them. kranepool has been doing just like usual, but like i've been saying, why not play him more? he's as good as we've got right now. despite sudakis' bat problems i have to think he strengthens us more than beauchamp. grote's been having problems but dyer has shown signs of life, like that marvelous two weeks back in when, june? so long ago, in happier days.

in the pitching, seaver will make his twenty somehow; koosman seems, finally, to be back, really back; mcandrew is the enormous gain; matlack has lived up to what they said, even with the heartbreakers he's lost from nonsupport. he's a terrific shot for rookie-of-the-year if he keeps going, or unless milner starts hitting homeruns a mile a minute. mcgraw and frisella are laboring a little but one assumes it's temporary. sadecki doesn't much matter at this point, except for a game or two he might pull for us, and rauch is an unknown quantity.

and if, and if. because if agee and staub both come back healthy they could mean eight or so games, which could be the edge we need.

when a heat wave breaks finally via a rolling thunderstorm—coming awake at six-thirty from fifteen minutes of nap and already feeling the changes, knowing from the force of the peals the air's getting cleaned, it's moving —and that night, later, there's a breeze in the living room at eleven when the game starts in san francisco.

then, in the middle of the game, pop, willie hit one, and it ain't that it makes old men feel young so much as that you just feel good, knowing how much he aches and still it went out. i don't expect any of my sons to root for willie or henry but i sure can. hang on, old men.

the heat wave breaks and for the first time in a week the bowels relax, your old lady touches you tenderly, despite all the hassling, the gnawing at each other. that's what it's all about, really.

even the baby, least affected by the heat because he was born to it almost a year ago, relaxes, smiles, can play happily instead of crawling always to the lap, the breast.

we are creatures of the weather and the year no matter how we try to change it.

tom seaver has no goddamned right blowing a god-damned ball game proving his goddamned machismo throwing a goddamned fastball to goddamned bobby bonds.

which leaves us one and two against both l.a. and s.f. in-stead of two and one. terrific. and now we're at the all-star break.

norman marshall bet me a dollar even on the american league. he won't pay it to me because he says earl weaver owes it. i agree it's weaver's debt, except that he owes it to norman, and norman still owes *me* the buck.

it wasn't so much the absence of sparky lyle that lost the game for weaver, as it was the pigheadedness of keeping wilbur wood in with a catcher what never caught a knuckleballer, and a man on third and no outs. he had a mess of pitchers on the bench with a million strikeouts between them including our own noley ryan. the boys here used to call him noley. god knows what they call him in california.

but what disturbed me most, i think, even more than last year, was the night-game aspect. i suspect i'll be bothered by it too, when world-series time comes round, since the middle three games are scheduled for the night. i don't want to sound romantic, but then i always do, and it seems to me that the very idea of the world series, and the all-star game, is that they are special things, played at a special time. and if you're working you plan if you can to go late to lunch so you can get a couple of innings in, or you have a radio hidden somewhere, or the messengers bring the word in, or even if you're not working in an office it's a weekday and so maybe you're in a plain bar like smith's on thirteenth and university with a bunch of strangers yelling like hell. last year i was in michigan for the game, way out in the western end of the state, sitting in a college commons room with my son dan and a couple of kids from the poetry group. they were from detroit, they'd never ever seen clemente play. that was okay, but the afternoon would have been still better. this year norman and i sit here, and it's just another night game, no matter how we try to make it something special.

bring back the old days. damn it, there are some good things about traditions, and some reasons why they become traditions, honest.

in fact, you grow to love the adamant cubbies more and more each year as the attendance, night games and all, falls off and off in places like san francisco. and the players talk about what a pleasure it is to play by day, and never face the lights. it's worth a try—maybe the kids would start watching ball games again.

and if they wouldn't, like i've said before, if the game can't make it on its own, it fails. but at least it would fail the way it was best, in hot daylight, the sun the reason why you're out there playing in the first place.

13

A SHORT BREAK IN THE ACTION

one saturday night the phone rang around ten-thirty; an
outraged tony heyes was on the other end. he was at the
head and had just gotten the sunday *times* and discovered
nixon's all-star baseball teams. he wanted me to answer
it immediately. tony's outrage was kind of nice, since
he's an englishman, newly acclimated to american sports.
but he is a sportsman, in the best way, which means that
when he comes to a new country he starts digging the
games, instead of sitting around talking about how su-
perior soccer is to football. one reason it is good that he
does this is that he has been known to back his opinion
with a quid or two, and in those circumstances you bet
on the games available where you are and that means you
ought to know something about those games.

he also has dabbled in politics back in the old country and
i suppose there was a bit of british horror that a president
should involve himself at this level.

but he was quite right even if british. the list demanded
an answer, if only because our peerless leader in all his

wisdom made everything clear with unusual forthright-
ness by saying his all-star american league catcher between 1925 and 1945 was either mickey cochrane or bill
dickey. he also had his son-in-law davey do the research,
which smacks of nepotism.

thus, when merch walked up to me in the middle of a pre-
prandial ginger ale and asked me where nixon rated on
my all-time list of presidents i decided that was the direction to take. first of all red smith had already taken
care of the baseball list and the president's talents as a
sportswriter and, despite my promise to tony, i didn't
think i could, say, do that end of it any better. this is a
rare admission from a writer. secondly, the list itself
couldn't really be attacked, because it was a masterpiece
of the obvious, and as indicated by the aforementioned
catcher selection, where it had to, it equivocated. i started
to muse in terms of ethnic and geographical distribution
of selections to see if either the southern or the blue-collar
strategy was working, but i'm sure it was. so i went to
work on politics and government, having at least as much
right to that field as tricky dick does to baseball.

for justices of the supreme court prior to 1862 i like
either marshall or taney. norman marshall, who still owes
me one dollar because of the all-star game, is directly or
collaterally, i don't remember which, descended from
john marshall, although his family no longer has money
or power, and so much for honor by breeding, say i.
environment is all, it would seem. taney makes the list
because his name is pronounced tawny, a good enough
reason for any man.

my all-time favorite opponent since 1945 has to be adlai
stevenson, but not because of his sparkling wit. once in
1956 in that big cafeteria at burnside and jerome avenues in the bronx he was very damned decent to larry

bronfman when they happened to be using adjoining urinals. supposing it turns out to have been averell harriman? or that whoever it was wasn't decent but sloppy? larry, where are you?

henry stimson is my favorite secretary of state because he once bought a briefcase in my father's store, although i wasn't there at the time. norman cousins and madeleine carroll and albert schweitzer were also among the famous customers. i wasn't there for any of them either.

sam houston, although never actually elected president, is my favorite all-time president. he was not allowed to play because of then-current prejudice in regard to drinking, divorce, and living with indians. however, had he been permitted to run and win, i feel sure the civil war would have been averted, but that is neither here nor there.

i had asked nathaniel to help with advice in this matter but his philosophy in matters political seems to consist solely of something unspeakable that ought to be done to mr. nixon. it involves the roof of our building and is unspeakable because i don't want his name included on that master list of assassination suspects the fbi had, despite the distinguished company he would have. in any event, this notion was probably fed to nathaniel at that socialistic school he goes to, or else he picked it up in the gutter. i mean, after all, if sex is openly discussed at home, what else could a kid learn in the gutter except politics?

my own credentials are not much stronger than nathaniel's when it comes to that, since deep in my heart i still think roosevelt is *really* president, proving again the jesuits were absolutely right, since roosevelt in fact had me until i was fourteen. i can accept harry s truman, since he was hand-picked by fdr—even though i have solid evidence that he was hand-picked in order to screw henry agard wallace. i am still convinced that either harry s or henry a. could in fact raise a grassroots ground-swell and turn the 1972 ratrace right around. but we can't have everything we want in this life.

but now i'm neglecting the list. if andrew jackson had been able to move to his left on the seminole question there is no doubt in my mind that he would have been my next-to-greatest all-time all-star president. no one else comes close, so i will leave that slot open. contrary to popular opinion thomas jefferson was neither voltaire nor leonardo da vinci.

diplomats, however, are easier ever since that guy in the newspaper store told me that ben franklin "danced with girls and all even though he was old." it certainly, despite the "and all," beats the hell out of stuffing tens and twenties in stewardii's bosoms.

since all congressmen, speakers of the house, and heads of committees are now or forever were the same person, that choice becomes difficult too, but there is one stick-out senator. happy chandler's secretary's friend owed my father's partner a favor, so i got to see the all-star game in brooklyn in 1948. and as a note to would-be bill-roeders let me say that i think it was 1948 but i ain't looked it up and don't intend to. in my head i believe it was 1948 and that's the way it's going to stay. that was also the game in which i saw robinson and musial batting back-to-back and twelve guys have told me that didn't happen either.

the best come-back politician comes from congress: ms. jeanette rankin. i sure hated her in 1941, since i was not able, at eleven, to believe that even one person in the united states of america didn't want to kick the shit out

of the krauts. but in the great wheel that is life here
she is back with us, honored and revered and a leader.

most courageous is whichever adams it was that went back
to the house of representatives after having been president. you can see that i don't remember my american
history very well, but damnit the records there aren't
nearly as accurate as in baseball. i mean it's demonstrable
that branch rickey was a terrible manager, but there are
many closet presidents we can make a case of greatness
for. i happen to like martin van buren myself, for example, but if any fillmore or arthur people want to fight,
i will need time to prepare myself for the debate.

and the most unbelievable act by any president in the
history of the american idea is the preparation of this
list by richard m. nixon. i can't believe he actually wrote
the damned thing—i mean, he *is* the prez, despite the
fact that i don't want him to be. this is a curiously romantic view to take, i know, that there are some things
you just don't do if you're president, but i'm stuck with
it.

it's as if ike had actually written that parody of the gettys-
burg address as he might have given it that was circulating fifteen years ago. there is really something obscene
about someone parodying himself, and while we laugh we
smell death around us. and, as always, it is our own.

the one thing that was consistently right all through this
summer was the icelandic saga of our own bobby fischer
taking on the universe and boris spassky.

somewhere in paul goodman's much too-little-known
novel *the empire city* he tells the story of the poor jewish
new yorker who gets drafted, fucks up by the numbers all
through his basic training, is useless and hopeless as far

as both the army and himself are concerned. finally, shipped to guadalcanal, he is stationed alone, with a machine gun, in an indefensible position, while the rest of the army retreats. single-handedly he beats off the attack of the screaming little yellow men, killing thousands, saving the day and the front. after, as he is being congratulated by the generals, his old sergeant asks what changed him. at last, he says, i was in business for myself.

and wasn't this bobby? all his life, fighting momma, the schools, the chess structure, the russians, and now, glory be, the world, including roone arledge and cbs-tv's wide world of sports. in fact, the only one he didn't conquer was the obdurate *sporting news*, which with single-minded intensity refused to cover this world championship, or even mention it.

and i desperately wanted to quote the goodman story over and over in the discussions at the head, but kept my peace, out of cowardice, i'm afraid, having recently taken a few too many minority positions. one loses his zest for constant fights as one gets into one's forties, i discover, so i watched the matches in comparative silence. the lion's-head crowd, on the other hand, had taken a vociferous moral posture which was equivalent to earlier feelings about such as benedict arnold. how the two were equated i still don't know but people were really outraged by what they called his poor sportsmanship. (for me, the whole question was resolved, albeit a bit late, when fischer, having appeared not only on time but indeed early for a state dinner in reykjavik, said: this isn't chess, this is the president of iceland.)

what seemed clear to me was simply that fischer was intent on demonstrating the virtues of private enterprise to spassky, and if boris isn't sitting on his dacha right now terribly bugged because you just aren't allowed to be that crazy under socialism, then i miss my guess. in fact, one of the loveliest ploys i've heard about was fischer, who long ago converted from judaism, showing up in spassky's room wearing a yarmulke, because he had heard that the russians wouldn't let spassky wear one in public.

you know, this is the same country where it turns out the astronauts set themselves up cozy deals through the moon missions, and while everybody says they were certainly naughty, the general tendency is to forgive them because they don't, after all, make a lot of money, etc. it occurs to me that the only thieves that america dislikes are fischer and the baseball strikers, which should prove something about morality in this nation of entrepreneurs.

at the time, in the middle of the match, my main concern was that bobby in fact knew what he was doing, and would quit fucking around in time to let the games go on. he was proved right, of course, in his estimation of the russians' forebearance. but all the publicity and all the hoorawing brought to the fore educational tv's great coup, mr. shelby lyman and the daily chess show. shelby was worth turning on even when you didn't know if there was going to be a game. nobody having told him that it's impossible for one man to talk for five hours at a time on television, he blithely went ahead with what, to my mind at least, was the best sports coverage of the decade. i didn't much know what he was talking about most of the time, since i'm not really a chess head, having given up the game in my early teens, but shelby kept checking in with other experts, so that i was convinced i was getting the straight dope. i mean there was an interplay between him and his consultants that was refreshing, to say the least, since when gowdy or gifford or meredith or kiner expert on the air you feel like they've said the last word on the subject even if you personally disagree. but with lyman there was always someone popping up with another point of view, usually diametrically opposed.

we had edmar, on the direct line from the marshall chess club in new york, we had frank brady calling in from iceland, and we had the ticker, with the play by play. the ticker had a bell attached to it that sounded for all the world like the bell that you used to find attached to grocery-store doors, tinkling as you came in, tinkling as you went out. it rang every time a new move was coming in, and you could hear it behind the discussion going on. there were also assorted chess buffs and/or experts in the studio, sitting around thinking, and finally there was the producer who ran in and out with the latest data off the ap wire.

all this lent a fluidity to the program that was incredible and much-needed in the world of sports reporting. it was helped by the fact that chess has by its nature great gaps of time in between the action, so that the commentary did not interfere with anything. i mean, in football they keep running into the plays, and the only good bullshitting in baseball games takes place during rain delays, because the stories otherwise keep getting cut off by the next pitch. and the rain delays have a built-in boredom factor, since what you're waiting for is the rain to stop, which is a spectator sport even i can't get interested in.

in other sporting events, such as the convention, we had the spectacle of walter cronkite talking on and on while the votes were being counted, and although it indicates the simplicity with which i face life, i had thought the votes were what the convention was about. the interviews at the conventions also outdid tony kubeck in their ludicrosity, as for example when muriel humphrey and eleanor mcgovern had to explain why one was sad and the other was happy while the california vote was being counted.

in the chess coverage, the most perfect of television experiences, you could luxuriate in the debates, the anecdotes, the guesses, until you heard the little bell ding-a-linging and then you got thirty seconds of terrific hard-core action. it became addictive. about the only thing i've even seen that could beat the 24-hour-a-day newsticker on cable tv for steady watching.

then, too, there was a human factor, since the guys feeding the ticker couldn't seem to keep their p's and q's straight, so shelby et al. were kept in a constant dither as to whether, in fact, the move made could possibly have been the one we were told it was. quite often it wasn't.

well, so much for the coverage. as for bobby and the match, they too were eminently satisfying. my moral position was, as i've said, somewhat different from the rest of my fellows. i'd felt, way back in the forties, that ted williams, while he was on the field, had the perfect right to give the finger to anyone he wanted, and i was a child then. i see no reason now to change my stance. i must respectfully submit that i like men who fuck around within their framework—if they have demonstrated they can play better than the rest of the world. i mean, if fischer moved his pawns backward, that would upset me—or if he punched the referee without a good reason.

most people think of us americans as sports buffs who think the game is everything, but this business shows us only to be insufferable liberals with a parochial-school ethos beaten deep into our hides: good guys win. which

is nonsense of course because good players win and there's
no morality about that, thank god.

DOES FISCHER EVER ERR?

as mistakes are made even by
ted williams' bat, though rarely,
they are made, are to be enjoyed
if nothing else, sheer masochism.

was the pawn taken taken in
error is the question or did
he have a line? unspoken:
if the great plummet where
are we? they sit and watch and
have to find a line for him
or die. he fell, falling
tried to snatch the game.
there's nothing wrong with that.

that the world would like its
orbit every time exact, no
mistake, absolutely perfect.
he moves each time in voids
no satellites disturb, in which
even the act of our watching
intrudes, disturbs. that
is life, our watching, but that
does not make him wrong.

he tries harder than we
do for perfection and he
needs it less. we die when
mistakes are made and he
fights on. leave him alone,
in madness or sanity we will
never know as black holds off
the white as best it can.
make no mistake in this.
the world will not allow it.

14

in august the magic ran out, or more likely, it became obvious to me that i couldn't keep sending the waves out. nothing worked. if cleon came back and agee was close, fregosi and harrelson each came down with back problems. there comes a point at which the expenditure of energy just doesn't pay off—not that you work magic for returns, but that fans can, i believe, supply that kind of energy, and everything will come together and the team will take off. that happened in '69. there were hits that fell in, errors that we forced the other team to make, breaks that "just happened," that can be explained in no other way.

some fans need the stands to do it, some can do it at home, some just walk around carrying the team with them. but each has some point where his energy gives out, and all he can do is watch. on august 3, for the first time in my life, i left a met game before the end of it. in the seventh inning of a game against philadelphia i turned to john and said, okay, let's go. philly had jumped to a start with a denny doyle homerun, for christ's sake. denny doyle, in addition to possessing a name that would have been terrific in 1934 with the giants, had hit five homeruns in all his life.

but it wasn't so much that, nor was it norman's scoffing as he sat with us. i had promised myself i'd spend one game at shea with a dyed-in-the-wool american league fan, preferably a yankee fan, and norman was it. but norman is very big and very pushy and while i love him dearly he doesn't know when to let up, and so the game became a whole succession of horrors and wisecracks. but, like i say, even that wasn't it. it was that there was no zing, no excitement, no nothing. the mets played like zombies that day, and i rooted like a zombie, and i can't frankly blame one or the other, either way. what i do know is that i was, literally, sick and tired by the seventh inning and so was john, and so, despite norman's objections and catcalls, we left. norman still owes me a dollar on the all-star game, you'll remember. he did have a right to catcall, since the yankees were starting to move and there was a very real possibility that they would catch the mets in percentage, and worst of all, have a shot at the pennant. there are some things too awful to contemplate in the company of the enemy.

this whole question of the presence at the ball park is going to be a big hassle this winter, what with the pressure building to ban local blackouts on football games. my own totally unsubstantiated feeling is that, again, the big mistake is in how they read the pull of sports on people. by which i mean simply that if people don't go to see the giants or the jets because they can sit home and watch them, then it's a comment on the game itself. overall attendance at major-league baseball this year is higher again, and there's not only plenty of tv coverage but that coverage is getting better and better with cameras all over the park, and zoom closeups and replays and slow motion over and over. i mean you can literally see and understand the game better at home. but i still go to the ball park and so do millions of other people. because you can feel the game at the park. sure, you sit there wondering what the hell happened on that particular play at second because all you really saw was a cloud of dust and the umpire signaling out! and you wish like hell you could see it again up close. but meanwhile you've accepted the out sign and the game is moving on.

guys talk about walking through the tunnel in yankee stadium in april and seeing nothing but that green diamond and knowing summer is coming. i don't care what kind of color set you got, you'll never find that feeling on it.

or, as pete hamill's friend said when he took her to the garden to see her first live fight: they got living color! so i think we needn't worry about television interfering with a game's attendance unless the game itself can't make it.

meanwhile, on the field, in the real game, in the real season, there were very weird individual magics working, even if mine had stopped, as witness jim beauchamp's astonishing performance on august 21, his thirty-third birthday (!) in which he hit two homeruns, drove in three runs, and won us a game against houston. he repeated the performance the next night with another homer and another win for us. if he had sustained this type of performance over the whole of his career he would have about thirty lifetime homers instead of the nine he now has. understand, i don't mean if he did it every day, but every season. all of which couldn't obscure the fact that on august 22 with less than fifty games to go, the club was heading inexorably toward third, unless a miracle happened. but a miracle was not about to happen.

there was a beautiful bit to add to owners and baseball mystique. mr. griffith of the minnesota twins, scion of a distinguished baseball family, the kind of ownership that is and always has been an ornament to the game, came up with the notion of signing and pitching early wynn against the texas rangers when they came to minneapolis if and only if ted williams would then reactivate himself long enough to take a turn at bat, so they would both go in the record books as the only people to have played in five decades. the next day mr. griffith added, i suppose if i sign him and he pitches i'd have to pay him. end of bright idea.

meanwhile the yankees kept coming strong, so much so that pennant fever was striking all through the bronx in the last weeks of august. i was sitting around the bar most afternoons with my nose in my ginger ale and not to the grindstone. my ear was to the ground and what i kept hearing i did not like. first of all there were all the helpful comments like nick browne asking me how it felt to sign a contract for a book about the wrong team—as if there could be a "wrong" team in this context. that's like saying purple is a bad color. or joe trying to be helpful and telling me i really ought to get out to shea for some locker-room interviews because "the dissension out there is terrific!" what i'm trying to say is that there were vibrations around and i was getting all of them.

there was also a rising undertone from such predictables as norman, who would call me after every yankee win to "discuss" it, and the flack stuff in the papers, and increasingly louder holy cows from phil rizzuto. and there was serious stuff going on: jimmy wechsler, who had been known occasionally to root for the mets or the columbias in his otherwise political column, suddenly and without warning revealed that he had been secretly listening to yankee games, and hamill confided to me that he was toying with the idea of doing a piece on sparky lyle (is sparky a nickname for a grown or little man in 1972?). worst of all schlenk started to crow from his privileged position behind the bar at the head. by his own admission he has not watched a yankee game since 1964 or whenever the fuck it was that the yankees last won and now he tells me, wow, i watched last night and what a great game it was!

then i pick up the sunday *times* and find them quoting fritz peterson's five-year-old son. they ask him where he thinks the yankees will finish this year and he says chicago. what has nathaniel done for me lately? i'll tell you what he's done. while willie mays is sitting around waiting to have his knee checked, nathaniel is telling me how he made believe he was willie and got two hits. terrific, kid, except you're five years old and white and your glove's still too big for your hand. fantasy is fine, but it's got to be constructive is what all the books say.

so all i can do for myself is to set down the ground rules. during this season and all coming seasons i will accept abuse or crowing from the following yankee fans:

anyone under sixteen years of age whose father is a rabid met fan;
anyone claiming to be an "old" yankee fan who can show me used tickets for at least two yankee games a year for six of the last eight seasons;
any pre-1965 met fan who became a yankee fan sometime between november of 1969 and july of 1972 because he found himself in disagreement with the policies of the mets management.

the rest of you guys can just crawl back under your rocks or into your seats at dallas cowboy games. you have to hate guys who follow winners and subsitute expediency for party loyalty. i say all this simply because being a fan does demand a considerable amout of stick-to-it-iveness. and it isn't only in terms of supporting your team, but also of hating the enemy. as far as i'm concerned the yankees could finish dead last for another ten years and it still wouldn't be enough—at least let yankee fans get a little education in how it is to die with a team. all of them, as far as i can tell, are still, right now, in the "how could they do it to me" stage. when they settle down and accept the fact that most of life is just awful, then they can have, nay, they will deserve, a pennant—but not until then.

i also have to say that i hope you understand that this is not a reaction to the met's standing and/or injury list, because i sincerely hope i would be saying it even if we were twelve games in front. in fact, as must be obvious, in my head they *are* twelve games in front, because they ought to be. staub and jones are fighting each other at about .340, seaver and koosman are both close to twenty wins, and even gentry has won fourteen.

but some will say that i'm being irrational about the mets and so jump to the conclusion that what i'm saying about the yankees is equally insane. it's not at all. in fact there are some yankees i care for dearly, or at least think i could. i hope for a splendid show from swoboda for the rest of the season, now that they're beginning to play him, and i have to root for rob gardner, also late of the mets. hal lanier and alou and callison all learned to play ball in the big league, so i have to be pulling for them too. but don't tell me about the yankees as a soul team, or mr. houk as a humanitarian. in fact, if you take away celerino sanchez, where are they? and he only came up after great agonies of despair in the yankee front office. at least, rumor has it, the mets coolly turned down their shot at him. and in the end, anyhow, he just ain't billy cox.

i'll tell you something else: if god wanted us to be yankee fans he'd have made us all clean-cut and assured of our places in heaven instead of scruffy and a little bit fearful. i've got a third of a season to get through yet, so talk to me about willie, and about agee and garrett starting to hit finally, and about pittsburgh still going strong, or even about cedeno as superstar, but don't tell me about a team from the bronx. a little humility is good for the soul and god knows that if anybody ought to be humble it's a team from that borough. i lived there for four years once and all i got from it was three poems and a divorce. but that's another story, and this story is about being a fan, and that's all.

while stewing in those ominous yankee juices, my brain trust, which is ziegel, decided that it would be salubrious for me to see how the other team lives. how could i parade myself as a baseball fan, his reasoning went, if i was unwilling to go up to yankee stadium once during the season and watch them play? i could not argue with his logic, since, as i've said, on the surface i've always presented the picture of objectivity, no matter what passion bubbled below.

the date we picked was august 31. this was the first day all year on which the yankee record was better than that of the mets. vic and i had set the date several weeks earlier, but nevertheless the awareness that this was how it worked out up there set up very bad omens all around.

and since the new breed of yankee fan seems to me just as bad, as biased, and as violence-prone as the old breed, i was hesitant about wearing my mets cap up there, even though vic had promised me seats in the sun and the cap would be ideal for shielding my sensitive eyes. in fact, i was not only hesitant, i was chicken. so i wore the marvelous panama that helen had gotten me for our anniversary. i suppose i should have known that this would be a wrong move also, but i had to wear something, since sunstroke is bad anywhere, but like most ailments, it's much worse above fourteenth street.

in any event, of course, the combination of the panama with my general appearance was irresistible to the folks and i had no sooner settled in my seat than a classic new jersey boor spotted the hat and started spewing filth.

i am fully aware that i am what you could call unusual-looking and that i might indeed be considered by some, principally elderly female relatives, as either horrid or awful, but i need only say here that at shea stadium i am known, loved, and accepted.

there *was* a problem years ago back at the polo grounds when, one night, as david and i and a few other guys all with hirsute adornment were leaving, some of the private cops made some comments about gillettes and barbasol and so forth, but i wrote m. donald grant and got a lovely letter back assuring me that the mets appreciated all their fans and that he himself had personally spoken to all the employees about laying off.

the worst that ever happened at shea was being called buffalo bill in a very pushy way, but that, now that i think of it, happened during a jet game. and there was also a horrible double header with pittsburgh back in '67 that i don't count, because we lost both ends so drearily and sadly that anything went, and so when three drunken gentlemen were heard to comment that for christ's sake if you lit him on fire it would take three days to put him out, i took it as genuine wit appropriate to the circumstances. it wasn't until the fifth inning of the second game that it came out, and at that point it was more than reasonable.

now while this guy was being just plain vile i did not have a picture of my wife and kids in my pocket, so there was nothing really to say to stop him, but i did have a picture of one thurman munson. ziegel told me that he plays catcher and he plays it all the time, whereas the mets generally let dyer and grote take turns. i had the picture because nathaniel had dug out his baseball cards and picked this one and asked me to watch to see if he played.

helen had also wished me well at the game, but i think she was a bit confused, since that night, at dinner, she had asked me which game i had gone to, and was astonished when i said the yankees. the fact that we were having dinner with the swobodas at the time did not help matters too much, but we managed to gloss over it. however, vic swallowed a shrimp in hot sauce whole, which was, like they say, très amusant.

the trip to the stadium was uneventful. i am sorry to have to tell dick young that we were not murdered once on our way into or out of the stadium and that all the tires were still on john's car even though we left it in the stadium parking lot. but the sightlines in the stadium have not improved and the infamous pillars are still in everybody's way. bob smith and i once had season tickets to the giant games there and we were in the lower stand between first and home, which meant we were cattycorner to the end zone and we were behind one of the pillars. i could see as far as the twenty and he could see from the forty on, so we watched each game with marty glickman sitting between us. but it does beat the shit out of the astrodome. the scoreboard stays quiet anyhow.

unfortunately the game itself was a laugher, the yankees scoring five runs in the first two innings off a team which called itself the texas rangers. i was disheartened to note that i could not recognize one name on the entire roster with the exception of the manager and three coaches—or only two coaches if the hudson mentioned was not sid hudson, but i presume he was, since the rangers are the eight or ninth variation of the washington senators for whom sid hudson used to pitch back when i knew every name on every roster.

featured in this onslaught were two high, drifting fly balls to right field that ended up in the stands for home-runs. they were the kind of balls that are easily caught in shea stadium, which is evidently why the mets do not have any ballplayers who can hit high fly balls that drift anywhere.

they did have an innovation out there about which i have not yet figured out a position to take. public-service announcements come out over the loudspeakers in the form of long, polite treatises. one, for example, explained that while the management was delighted if you kept balls hit into "occupied areas" of the stands, they must insist that you not go onto the playing field or in any way interfere with the ball while it was in play. what has me puzzled here is that i think i like simpler policy statements, even if mean and inhuman, rather than long, involved explanations which somehow end up more menacing.

there was also a splendid announcement concerning the nice young ladies in low-cut red blouses who were circulating through the stands. they don't go in for that sort of thing out at shea and i must say i liked it. i think one of them smiled either at me or with me, i'm not sure which.

the mustard at yankee stadium is yellow, which is a sign that they haven't lost their goyishe tam even if they did manage to hire blomberg. in any event a large jewish boy from atlanta, who doesn't even know how to pronounce his own name or else spell it if the pronunciation is correct, probably likes yellow mustard. has anybody ever checked, officially, to see if he's indeed circumcized? i'll tell you one thing. art shamsky liked brown mustard.

they also have robert merrill singing the national anthem, but for some unknown reason they start the record with a reprise of the last bar, so you have to stand longer than at shea. however, i am happy to report that rumors of more intense patriotism at yankee stadium than at shea are grossly exaggerated, since everybody starts whooping it up for the game at just about the same point in the middle of the star-spangled banner.

on this note i might add that raymond, the city college bagelman, was out in the parking lot selling, and when vic introduced me to him as a city college professor he promptly informed me that mcgovern would ruin the country.

the american league umpires use outside chest protectors. this is the only instance of total class at the stadium i am able to report, and that's not their decision, it's a league rule. there's something wonderful about an umpire shifting his chest protector around that is sadly lacking in national league games.

and sparky lyle does, in fact, have really long hair, so i guess mike burke is trying. i was trying, too, but, honest, there's just no way i can grow to love the yankees.

special thanks are due to ziegel for managing to submerge his true heart, which, having grown to maturity within a few short blocks of yankee stadium, put up in silence with the abuse heaped on the yankees. he may be the only yankee fan i can find it in my heart to love, and he's entitled to a winner. ten years from now.

15

the olympics came crashing in as expected, and although they ended on horror, up until that dreadful point they were in fact fun and games, with much gaiety and merriment about the games themselves, the coverage, and the fuckups of the american officials. i never got myself to the typewriter about all the foreplay because the murder of the israelis swallowed quite properly all those considerations, but i had been greatly taken by a couple of things. i wondered, for example, why all the people screaming about the black irreverence shown on the winners' platform never once bitched about the girls' relay team which did just as much bopping on the platform during their solemn moment. of course they were young and happy and white.

and i also swelled with pride at larry young's performance in the fifty-kilometer walk—already being taken, as you will understand, by weirdo events like that. i used to get freebies to the track meets at the garden and i sort of fell in love with the walk then—it really is the only race that you can watch strategy developing in, and you learn to put up with the curious movement. i mean if guys can get excited about the high hurdles, certainly there's room in the world for a strange kind of walk.

but there was an embarrassment, it seemed to me, about young's bronze medal—as if it were somehow shameful that an american should be able to do well in such an event. the marathon carried with it the weight of centuries, so that was somehow acceptable, but even there there was a little wonder. i mean i really believe that no one could accept the fact that we were out in the dashes and the middle distance and the field events and in, in walking twenty-six-mile runs and chess. the world turned topsy-turvy as the british played while they stacked their guns at the great surrender.

LONG DISTANCE

larry young did
big daddy call? did
the telephone ring in
your lonely head? with
beard and cap and "shades
and baggy shirt," from
the same hometown as
harry s truman, "who
also liked to walk," in
that "lonely sport no one
pays any attention to
here," what could he
say to you? could he
tell you you were not a
flower of your place and
time? could he say children
should not emulate you?
or that you ought to
settle down, get a job?

who, after all, could use
the third best thirty
or so mile walker in the
whole wide world, and
what could you do for us?

on tuesday, september 5 the olympics finally died in the
blood of seventeen people. i would not have written that
line that day, but now, some time after, it seems clearer
and clearer that that is precisely what happened—even if
there are new games at montreal. the simple fact is that
the games have foundered in a sea of nationalism and
commerce and that it's no longer possible for a man
simply to try to outdo his fellow man in a physical con-
test. vince matthews climbed fences to practice for an
event they said he was too old to qualify for, and he won
it, and he was damned because he did his shuffle during
the playing of a national anthem he had enough reason
to believe was not his.

but that's putting it on too personal a level. it strikes too
many chords in too many people black and white, and indeed, it strikes at all countries. what could the russians
say about a man who claimed it was his legs that won
him a gold medal and not the power of a great nation?
and yet it seems to me that this is the only legitimate concern of the olympics, but then i'm an anarchist in this
as in other matters.

nationalism has always controlled the olympics. much as
i might approve, for example, of the action of the black
nations in threatening a boycott of the games if rhodesia
was allowed to compete, in the end that was a "national-
ist" response to all the nationalism that went before. and
the nationalism, abetted by the ever-growing influence of
the host nation's commercial interests and the tremen-
dous investment by television, has laid the games low,

and indeed, laid them open and vulnerable to such horrors as the massacre of the israeli athletes. of course, i know that the black septemberists were by any criteria madmen. but how in the world could they have conceived of such an outrageous act if not for the fact that it was inextricably tied to an internationally prestigious and totally available competition of nations? a weightlifter straining at his barbells in his own name is no man's target except the man straining next to him, the man waiting in the wings, the kid growing up, dreaming. the israeli weightlifter is the target of anyone who wants to hurt israel for whatever reason, just as i by my very appearance am a target of any black who hates whitey or any hardhat who hates long-hair freaks. i am no longer allowed to be joel oppenheimer, nice guy and good poet and father and husband and mets fan.

avery brundage could not let go, even at the memorial services, of the abstraction of the games. to him, an old man, the boycott and the murders and matthews' disrespect were all of one piece. they threatened the olympics, and that could not be allowed.

there was in all this the further complication of the setting: the west germans trying so hard to create a new image, to not be "german," as the world had come to characterize them in the last one hundred years.

and so seventeen people died violently, and only eight of them had some sort of choice. moshe weinberg and joseph romano *decided* to try to resist and were killed for it; and five members of the arab nationalists group and one west german policeman died as a result of their violent calling. the other nine israeli hostages died without options. nothing can change these terrible facts.

there has followed an equally terrible campaign of letter bombs, a series of "small" strikes by the israeli government, and a continuing controversy within and without the olympics as to the awarding of medals and the banning of athletes for misbehavior. doesn't it sound as horribly macabre as it is when they run in the same sentence?

i am trying to talk here, after the fact, but in the midst of life, about decisions and priorities and national concerns and abstractions.

golda meir was presented with a list of terrorist demands and decided not to compromise. in the bar they called her a ballsy woman.

the west germans made a decision to try to pick off the arabs. they used five snipers and shadows. the snipers missed.

abc and cbs had a hell of a time making decisions as to who should get to use the satellite to bring the "news" to us, and that decision finally hinged on which level of executive should write which begging note to which other level of executive.

i am in no position to comment on the reasons for making these decisions one way or the other, since i am responsible neither for the continued existence of israel nor the image of germany nor the nielson rating of abc or cbs, but i do know that in these circumstances there is no decision at all that could be "correct."

the statement should be obvious, because, simply put, these decisions were all made by people in one place about people in another. there were some decisions made by the people involved: the norwegians going home because they believed the games had been resumed for purely commercial reasons, the egyptians going home for fear of reprisal. even the athletes who continued playing ping-pong while the horror went on may have made the right decision, for what would you have had them do? perhaps they should have lined the fences with the rest of the spectators? possibly, even, the terrorists made the right decision, to strike in this way at this place at this time. if the history books tell our grandchildren so, it will be so.

what i am angry about is this obvious declaration that old men continue to make decisions. nothing the young can do can be worse than the mistakes that old men have made year after year, century after century, second after second. we live with those mistakes and they are made out of reason, they tell us. the young are honest, at least. they murder when they do out of madness or despair or the illogic of fun. but the young men are fueled by the decisions laid on their heads, whether it be the young madmen, the young jocks, or the young dead fucked up in their head by junk and war and hopelessness.

we are supposed to be passing on wisdom and understanding, and since we have none we pass on technology and progress and still everybody breathes a sigh of relief when we make a "decision." it smacks of something being done, of giving us a road to follow. the police sniper who fired the first shot that triggered the final holocaust thought he had a stab at it. he was wrong, but that was precisely the decision he had been put there to make.

and yet it is silly to ask that death be bigger than the olympics or than nations. we so desperately and perhaps properly fear death that we want anything to be bigger than it. as *a.m. new york* was covering the initial reports from munich a young lady called in. she said: i went to sleep last night and i woke up this morning and all this was happening. it was a very simple, very human, and very stupid plea. it asked that the world go on without the world's interference, as you ask and i ask and we have always asked.

or, like the young canoeist said while being interviewed on her arrival back at kennedy: we were way over at the other end. we didn't know what was going on.

we will never again, i think, be allowed this luxury we've enjoyed of so totally watching, simply and with care, a man falling down while trying to lift more weight than any man before him, or trying to run faster than any man in the world, or even, that most primitive of sports, trying to beat another man up. we will never have this circus any more, really, except in small places where small boys try to stretch themselves. that will go on eternally.

the world is complaining about the jocks, the world talks snidely now about the runners who worried about their training, their loss of condition, while men were dying. but i would ask what, ever, has the juggler been able to present to our lady but his skill?

consider this carefully, because there are so many others for you to judge. judge those who cry for vengeance and those who turn their faces. judge those who grin with the terrorists, although i do not believe the terrorists themselves grinned, i believe in this they were serious. judge those who call for guns to protect us from them or them from us. judge the wise rabbis who will draw the wrong lessons from this terror, because they have lost the voice of god, the word of god. judge the commentators who push and haul the universe until it fits their idea of it— and if, writing now, i am one of those commentators, judge me, for god's sake.

let us have done with horseshit! abc switched to volley-ball for just a second during the morning, to show us that the games were still in progress, those parts that had already got under way. then jim mckay said: i guess we'd better go back to the real world, if that's what it is. you bet your sweet ass it is, jim. not that i'd choose it, but what else could it be? the real world where simpletons pick out one simple thing to try and do well while the geniuses make decisions.

my decision is that i have only the following wisdom and understanding—security is a game, governments are a game, and unless you know this, you too are a game. pheidippides ran the twenty-six miles because he was hired to do a job he could do better than anyone else around. it was a message about men killing other men, and he died carrying the message. of the soldiers and the runner, who died best?

POST-SEASON
AND WINTER BALL

16

now they start hitting! it's september 14. last night the mets won their fifth in a row and the first four men went ten for eighteen, knocked in six runs and scored nine. and staub, agee, and mays weren't in the lineup! boswell, pursuing his stated aim of "getting over .200," went four for five. cleon knocked in four runs on three hits to become the first met with fifty runs batted in. i know it was off philly, but i sat and relaxed with it. it was the longest game of the year according to the news this morning, and it was so nice.

during the game i got a call from a young teacher who had taken umbrage about my piece on yankee fans and written me more in sadness than in anger. now he wanted to talk about a visit to his writing class and when i said i was watching us win, like all yankee fans he only knew about his club's loss. well, says i, think of it this way: we're fighting for second and you guys may be fighting for fourth. i liked it so much that i kept trying norman until he got home from the stadium. he had gone out last night and the night before, and after the first game, which the yankees won, he'd called about eleven-thirty and spent a half-hour breaking my balls, so turnabout was like they say. now norman was down on mets fans, who he claims are fat-cat, comfortable burghers, and non-sportslovers. some of them are, i keep telling him. he swears he's going to kill one the first time he sees someone try to pay for a hotdog with a credit card. but i tell him yankee stadium is the only place i've been put down for hair, etc., in five years—and that includes fights at sunnyside (where there was a good deal of amused astonishment and awe, but no badmouthing) as well as the garden and shea. met fans, i tell him, know that our father's house has many mansions, so they ain't hard-asses. he claims, on the other hand, that yankee fans are true fans, street people, etc., and their first impulse is to come on strong to someone they don't understand. i say fuck'em.

but the young teacher was more reasonable than norman. he wanted to know if i meant i really wasn't rooting for the yankees, deep down, and i could hear him shrivel when i said that deep down i was hoping they'd finish last again. but in fact he was so hurt that i had to go into a long thing about how hidden in my hate was a real love, because how could i hate them so hard if they weren't a new york ball club? i told him how the football giants don't exist for me any more, how in the bar i either say i've never heard of them, or call them the hoboken giants or the swamp giants, or i talk about the giants being a club in the western division of the national league. they don't exist is the simple fact. it's really kind of pleasant watching reactions, because and awful lot of guys look me straight in the eye and tell me how they've given up their season tickets, but they're still following them, because the habit is too strong. it's a little like the looks from guys who think they ought to stop drinking instead of just cutting down, when they see me with a ginger ale. meanwhile, i'm just playing my own game, which is to set my own limits on the world of sports, just like the games set their own limits on possibilities there.

i won't mention that we had to use four pitchers, and that, for once, matlack having gotten some runs, he was bombed all over the lot—nine hits, five runs, three walks in three-and-one-third innings. which is too bad, because all we can hope for now (like boswell, i guess) aside from second-place money, is working on the stats. like, it would be nice if milner got to the 270's, cleon to the 280's, matlack and mcandrew, and, much as i hate to say it, seaver, win a couple more. who can we get for gentry next year? and the other big news was that tidewater goes to the little world series, having won its play-off, and tommie moore is coming up for a couple of games. he had a no-hitter with them this year to match the one for memphis last year, so i presume we have another hot young pitcher to root for next spring. well, hell, they were right about matlack—and they might still be right about capra.

today is an off day, traveling to chicago, for which thank god, since it's opening day at city college as far as i'm concerned, and i was afraid i'd have to sweat out this crucial series in class. hell, if the yankees are going to go crazy so can i. and i'm waiting to see what kind of crowds we get on the last home stand, since those vaunted yankee fans that norman keeps yelling about when faced with a chance to put boston away in a midweek night game showed up about fifteen thousand strong. that's ridiculous. norman, of course, said that they were all real fans. well, like queen mary's chauffeur said to queen wilhelmina's chauffeur when they met in the rolls and the daimler facing each other on a one-lane road, what is this, a five-pound bag of shit?

so we shall see what we shall see in chicago. of course, all season, these are the series that we've dived on. maybe it changes now, despite seaver's pain in the gluteus maximus. it would be nice to see, and then they're talking about staub coming back for the last home stand. and don't forget willie and agee, who seem to like wrigley field. something about the ivy, no doubt. henry aaron hit two last night to bring him up to thirty. it's still going to be a long haul. that place on the all-time list is important to me—like the finish in the marathon with wolde at forty finishing third. if the belgian hadn't snuck in, he'd have been second, and a "twenty-eight-year-old writer from oregon" would have been third. that would've been perfect. in any event, the season is now, as i've said, statistics.

would it be out of order after all this to point out that the mets were finally and irrevocably erased from the 1972 pennant race on the eve of yom kippur? the season did start or didn't, as you prefer, on that conjunction of easter, april fools' day, and passover, and as passover is the promise of the spring, so is yom kippur the time for summing up, the time to look back on your sins of the last year. and so the mets lost to chicago, 6–4, in one of those stupid herky-jerky affairs they have been specializing in: down two-nothing on a bad beginning by mcandrew, who then straightened out but had his ribs start hurting again, followed by sadecki, who pitched well but then gave up two tainted, like they say, runs, followed by mcgraw, who was presented with three runs by the mets, and then gave up two himself, so that the mets, having been out of it and back in, went up to bat in the ninth down three and the heart presumably out of them and got another run, and then with a man on base milner drove one far back to the wall that billy williams, damn

146

him, chased and waited and timed his jump and pulled it down, and we lost another.

but not as bad as the two days before. we went into chicago two out of second, with a five-game winning streak, and gentry got killed in the first game—and also, following the master again, came up with his own pain in the ass, so that presumably he and seaver can now fight over the whirlpool. and on saturday seaver got his worst beating ever—18–5, which is also the worst new york has ever taken, fifteen walks, a grand-slam homerun by hooton, my god, how bad can it get? the only thing that saved me was helen's shopping list. for reasons that are, i'm afraid, far too transparent, the approach of yom kippur seemed to trigger deep insecurities in her as far as food supplies went, so that i had not only the supermarket shopping in the morning, to which i'm used, and, indeed, enjoy, but also a large run to balducci's vegetable market for roots and leaves in such quantity that the other shopping had to be made on a third trip.

i had also promised the kids that i'd take them to the perry st. fair, and i did that along with the third trip. you know already that i don't usually let commitments to nathaniel interfere with the game, but i could hardly avoid taking him to a street fair which was exactly four blocks away, and besides i had some idea, after friday, that the mets didn't want me to watch them. they sure didn't, and so i had some peace, and a little hope, until i walked into the yard here and young matthew came running up with the news that we lost. what was the score, i asked in all my innocence, and he as innocently answered. to ten-year-olds one loss is the same as another and i have seen kids in all honesty miss a goldfish as much as their grandmother, but it hurts to be old and vulnerable and swinging along in a mets cap, let me tell you. lem right now is at that perfect age where he cries as long as it hurts and laughs as long as it pleases him and that's that. he hasn't yet learned the terrible maturity which consists in holding hurts and pleasures far beyond their usefulness.

so, one hopes the crisis of the seasons has passed. the mets returned to new york with seventeen games to go and a possible vague shot at second, and opened against pittsburgh monday night. matlack went all the way, pitched a shutout (against pittsburgh! his second!) and staub returned to the lineup, got two hits, raised his average over .300, scored the winning run, and what can i tell you? it figures. and don't tell me about pittsburgh not caring—they're slumping, finally, and i'm sure they'd like to be waltzing home instead. like getting themselves up for the play-offs? not to mention that the mets are now two up on the season series, and if we end up ahead in that, now that staub is playing again, don't you think everyone, me included, is going to talk about how we would've killed them if we'd only stayed healthy?

you bet i would. we played 36–22 with him and 36–47 without him, and without the rest of the guys in and out as they were for two months inside his three months. well, i said, yom kippur is when you look back at the year and consider your sins, and i have decided it was an act of hubris, pride before the gods, which was the key sin. as erich segal would be glad to tell you, hubris was the worst as far as the greeks were concerned and in this case i find it sadly prominent in the hiring of willie. now let me explain before you all start screaming: simply that m. donald, i have come to believe, took willie on as either an act of mercy to an old man, or strictly as a public relations stunt, depending on which jaundiced view of the universe you prefer to hold. if they had bought him because we needed him, or could have used him—which the gods in their wisdom decreed was the way it should turn out—then none of this would have happened, and willie would be chafing, and getting in now and then, and being a hero every time like he was at the beginning, and lindsey nelson would still be raving about his fantastic on-base percentage, and we would be fifteen games in front, with everybody hitting like hell, and the pitchers all up in the high teens, except for tom, who would have his twenty-five already. now do you understand? you can't screw around with the gods, fellas. or like the little man three inches tall said, never call a witch doctor a mother-fucker.

meanwhile, instead of all those good things to talk about we have bob murphy shining through by talking about the beautiful indian summer on september 18, which by my calendar is several days ahead of the end of genuine summer; and the other day they got into a statistical rap concerning the fact that the mets have never ever fin-ished third! They finished first and second, and indeed, tied for third, but never just all by themselves in third. now isn't that terrific, and a new met record to aim for. i say it's spinach, and i say to hell with it.

now that i think of it, i have no way to check except to listen to tapes all the way through the season and i ain't about to do that, but it seems to me these excesses really happen on the nights when there's no television—so they get this desperate feeling about filling up air time. i don't know that for a fact, but the television gaffes seem to oc-cur less frequently or to be on a less serious level. they're just ridiculous most of the time. these are evil. i mean, should we try for fourth next year just to fill up that slot in the record book?

and for another record, will we end up this season with the most untradable players? i mean the one possibility that someone might want that we should be able to spare

149

is jerry grote, who seems to have worked himself out of a job, or at least dyer worked himself in (again, he knocked in staub last night, and he's hitting around .250 with, like they say, power and that's twenty-five or so points over his lifetime, and he's catching good). the only hitch is that we now got no back-up catcher in the minors. i think all the guys at tidewater hit around .225, which is just terrific. so we got to keep an unhappy grote on the bench just in case something happens to the duff. then we have the gold dust twins in gentry and jones, either of whom would have brought nice things during last winter—like nate colbert for gentry, i keep getting sick remembering. now the only problem is how to sneak them into pittsburgh so they can fuck up their locker room—at least that's what the boys in the press keep writing about. one bitching, the other goofing. and harrelson for sanguillen, which was also a juicy item last winter? well, now we got no infielders left, remember? unless they'll take boswell and garrett and fregosi and we put sanguillen on third. why not?

the weather has turned around. just one night after murphy declared indian summer, the fall came swooping in. it was pleasant all morning and early afternoon but by five-thirty or six the wind was sweeping through the house, nathaniel'd been home all day with the beginning of his fall cold, and at that we were lucky, since last year it started august 20 (and went 'til january 15), but the house was really freezing, so we bundled him up. later after dinner, sitting watching the second pirate game at shea with the dobbses over, i almost said something to john about maybe taking the ladies to thursday's night game, but decided to let it go. it's too late, perhaps, for night games, and all in one day.

and this morning reading the *sporting news*, i see there's a guy worrying what singleton is going to do next week at montreal against the mets, since they finally nailed his allergy down to wool uniforms. he got special permission to wear double-knits, which proves you can fight city hall if you got a medical excuse. anyhow he's hitting .343 since the day in july when they finally discovered it was the uniform that had fucked him up. as a matter of fact the *sporting news* piece was concerned with what a great trade the staub deal was for montreal. well, it was a great one for us, too, but we may never know it. staub got two hits last night, i believe—i haven't checked the papers yet, but before his last at bat he was up to .307. dreams of glory, of what might have been. look on these wonders and despair. cleon broke out of his slump with a single right after staub finally *didn't* get on base, so it was a classic ninth inning. it was a classic game, in fact: pittsburgh six runs on seven hits, mets one run on six hits.

in any event, why take the ladies to the game, you may well ask, or else questioning with piercing, glittering eye, why not take the ladies to the game? well, i'll tell you. helen don't really care much for baseball, although she'll settle for any evening out. but she really likes basketball, where you can watch the men in their underwear. ann dobbs, on the other hand, went to her first game last week up at yankee stadium, john having promised michel he'd take him once this season, which in turn incidentally led to nathaniel forcing a promise out of me for next season, although i had said originally that he would wait 'til ten, but six is what i've promised, so six it will be. somehow john's promise to michel turned into a promise to ann, michel's friends gibby and michael and marko, and off they went. and ann fell in love. but not only with the game, also unfortunately with the yankees. so then we thought we ought to take her out to shea, and i broached the idea to helen. she pleaded inertia, thinking i meant yankee stadium. she flickered a bit when i said no shea, but i really got the feeling she could live without either. so now the weather has us off the hook. i think. i suspect i will hear about this some dark day in november, somehow it will be stuck in me that we never went to the game i promised her. screw that. can you plan your life around what your wife is going to yell at you in november about? i suppose you have to. or else learn the hard way.

the season ended. the mets were severely ensconced in third place and about the only thing that could be said was that their percentage was better than the yankees. praise god for small blessings. norman can only bug me about lyle vs mcgraw, but since one finished first and the other a close third (with clay carroll in between), in relief stats that's not a bad fight. matlack was great, milner slumped off and on, but considering the pressures i'm more than satisfied, and i hope they are. willie paid off. will he be back? who knows? it would be nice if he could get another season in, this time just for fun, playing with a healthy team.

i figured up the much-maligned bench and they came in at .229, which is four points better than the team as a whole. it ain't much, but it makes me happy, because i thought under the circumstances they did a fantastic job.

the circumstances are there in the stats also: not one met with 440 at-bats, which is the *sporting news* break-off point for qualifying for batting records. kranepool was in the most games, an awful lot of which were as pinch-hitter or for half the game before being pulled for a pinchhitter, and he was only in 122, and everybody else was in less than three-quarters of the schedule. the only clubs anywhere near this level of inconsistency were ones like los angeles, which deliberately wanted a platoon, and san diego, which also did it out of desperation but didn't have a starting eight to begin with.

there was no power on the club, but that's staub, agee, and jones. the pitching held up surprisingly well given the lack of support. they were fifth in era.

where do we go from here? that depends on whether you have given up on gentry, jones, agee, boswell, garrett, or any of the above. there is much talk of more trades. i've lumped them all together, because it gets wacky and nice. even better than last year's harrelson for sanguillen:

seaver to pittsburgh for cash, may, clines, and walker.
gentry and grote to atlanta for millan and williams.
harrelson to st. louis for torre.
beauchamp, boswell, fregosi, and garrett, or jones and agee to san diego for colbert.
fregosi to california for ryan.

the first of course is defensive, because if pittsburgh is indeed willing to give all those guys for carlton they would certainly give them to us for seaver, and the other way, both clubs get stronger, and indeed philly becomes a threat immediately.

the second is likely, except that everybody is leery about grote's throwing since the operation.

the third is two years too late but what the hell, could it hurt?

the fourth is my invention, and it certainly does give san diego an infield or an outfield, doesn't it?

the fifth has been much mentioned ever since california's statement that they would give up some pitching for a hitting infielder. i love it.

we'd then have the following squad:

c: williams, dyer, may.
of: staub, milner, mays, jones, agee, marshall, clines.
if: martinez, millan, cash, barnes, torre.
ib: colbert, kranepool.
p: mcandrew, matlack, koosman, walker, ryan, mcgraw, frisella and whoever.

you'll notice that kranepool is one of my untouchables.

but it's all nonsense, because i'll do as i have done, and live or die with the squad they give me.

i won't even talk about the play-offs and the series. my heart just wasn't in them, even though the games, for the most part, were beautiful—maybe, abstractly, the best i've seen in a long time. but that was the point. it was abstract. who could root for oakland *or* cincinnati? pittsburgh or detroit had a little bit of a hold on me, but despite oakland's hair and epstein and holzman, and despite the fact that cincy is national league, there were too many things working against them. first of all, i hate bench and rose. don't ask why because i don't know. there is only one thing that could make me love them and that obviously is a trade to the mets. as to oakland, when i heard gertrude stein's quote, "there's no there there," i felt absolved of any need to worry.

so the wrong season ended for me with a whimper. seaver's twentieth irritated me this year instead of saving the season like it did last year. the season ran too long, way into october, and then jackie robinson died.

17

the season which started with april fools' day and the
death of gil hodges, and ended for the mets with yom
kippur, ended for all of us with the death of jackie robinson right after the world series. jack robinson ran the
bases fast as you can say. he was born in georgia, a football hero in california, an officer in the war to save democracy. heywood hale broun said it all in his eulogy:
he was a classic hero, and like all classic heroes he
carried with him one flaw imposed by fate. he was black.
as surely as oedipus or any of them, his flaw destroyed
him, crippling him, blinding him, killing him at fifty-
three as sadly as with oedipus or any of them, why was
his flaw a flaw?

by his talents and his forbearance and his flaw baseball
was changed forever. it was at a time when we believed
the rest of the american game would change too.

in any other universe his life would, perhaps, have not
been terribly different, but it would at least have been

happier. and the rewards, that came to him would have been enjoyed in the peace that should have accompanied them. he was smart, healthy, and handsome. he ought to have lived in that other universe. where he also would have been less driven, less beset.

and we who cried when we heard of his death, we who write or speak these eulogies, we might, then, not have noticed, or might have merely mentioned it in passing. because good men of great ability die every day in this world and there are not enough tears. but men, not symbols, die in such a quiet way.

my generation was young when robbie started; in 1947 i was seventeen, and that was very young in those days. i stood in the stands the day he came to brooklyn and i was surrounded by black faces. that had never happened to me before. from somewhere near me i heard a voice from childhood, a jewish tailor. yankel yankel yankel he yelled, as hard as all his neighbors shouting jack jack jack. that is very hard to believe this year when his children live in forest hills.

they tell me jack was not a gentle man; did they expect ernie banks smiling all day long? it takes a long time to enjoy what you are fighting to hold onto—and i mean no disrespect to banks, it's just that i think by now we don't call superstars nigger. in 1947 we did.

what died here with jackie was an era, gasping now these five or ten last years until now it's running out totally. and he marks its end as well as any could. it was a time when young people hoped and old men realized, or at least began to realize, they could no longer stop that hope, and began to give a little. that time has ended because the young are old now, because every one is scared, because the world is scared.

and so we won't see him rounding third again, or dancing down the line, except in films—startling enough to stop conversations, draw your eye inexorably to the image, even if you don't care—or as i had to tell philip, too young to remember, they had to invent the split screen to cover him on first, which is perhaps today's measure of the importance of the man.

the lashing out will grow worse and keep on growing but the day of his death was marked by a school bus attacked, teachers robbed in their classrooms, and yes, two ponies beaten to death by kids. we won't talk about what happened that day in the election campaign or what they call the government, the higher levels.

we won't even talk about adrian constantine "cap" anson, who single-handedly kept baseball pure for whites for nearly a hundred years; we won't even talk about richard m. nixon, who had the arrogance to put leroy "satchel" paige on his all-time all-star team because he would've been great if he could've played. and we certainly won't talk about the brooklyn fans who booed robbie's first error as if it proved them right. we will talk about the stance, the bat held high, the head looming, and the ball bouncing off the wall in deep left center, and the crazy garbage truck run, the pigeon toes.

and in a world where he was clean, and where, yes, dixie walker was clean too, with his long-bred hatred, and the point for both was to score the runs and make the flashing play, in that same world, we will continue dirtying ourselves by our hopes, our lives and our leaders.

i had tried to tell myself i would not tie all this together, but how can i not? did america deserve jackie robinson? i think it didn't, and i know for sure that jackie deserved better than us. all winter long you do statistics. it's what saves you, when the dry time is here, like now, monday-night football. a basketball game now and again. or hockey. you sit with the library:

daguerrotypes, the records of the all-time all-stars
the macmillan encyclopedia
the baseball register

these you have to have. then there are all the paperbacks, some with one statistic you need, some with another. personally i'm mad at fawcett's "official major league baseball records" because it led me to believe it would carry on-base percentages and didn't. but it's really handy. the point is to dig up trivia questions for the bar: going into 1972, take bob gibson, fergy jenkins, and juan marichal. tell me (a) best-win-lost percentages, (b) lowest era, (c) most twenty-game seasons. ha-ha, marichal to all three. too bad i'm not drinking. but then you also keep figuring things to justify last year, or hope for next year. i use "runs produced average" (rbi plus runs scored minus homeruns, per at-bats) and, for the team, team run production (rbis per hits, and rbis per bats). if you contrast the two team averages with the pitching staff's era, you ought to get a picture of where the club stands relative to the others in its division. of course you can get that by looking at the team standings, but this is more fun—and it also tells you interesting things about the clubs. i worked it out for the mets and found out they were getting, relatively, good run production, and they had, as usual, despite gentry and koosman and frisella, a good era. they just weren't getting many hits or at-bats. see what i mean?

anyhow, i was doing the dishes last night, it was a monday, and wins was on as usual, and i got sad because there was the damned monday-night football game, and nothing else. and i started thinking about how it's pretty

dark these mornings getting up around seven, and again
i wondered how i'd make it through the winter without
baseball to hang onto, without the sun to hang onto. because that's the point, in the end, that they're both tied
together for me, and i'm sorry, but when it's dark early
in the afternoon and dark late in the morning, and all
they're playing is football and hockey and basketball,
something inside me draws into that tiny knot that my
shoulders make in january when the wind is coming off
the river. i used to say i hibernated from thanksgiving to
groundhog day and i believe that in a very real sense i
do. all the attention is inward—vide the statistics, pure
headgames—whereas the spring and summer the eyes
peer out.

so, while the winter sports drone on, i watch, but i don't
watch. i do teams, maybe:

ripper collins, 1b, 9 yrs	.296/.492
eddie collins, 2b, 25 yrs	33/428 (hall of fame)
hub collins, ss, 7 yrs	.284/.369 (faking it—he played 2b and of, and only 20 games at short —but i'm sure he could've)
jimmy collins, 3b, 14 yrs	.294/.410 (hall of fame)
shano collins, of, 16 yrs	.262/.362
joe collins, of, 10 yrs	.256/.421 (i'm pushing again, but he did have 114 games in the outfield, and not even a yankee fan would move the ripper for him)

159

rip collins, of, 1 yr*   .271/.358 *(he was, of
                                             course, a su-
                                             perb pitcher,
                                             but in 1922 he
                                             played   117
                                             games in the
                                             outfield, and i
                                             need him)

pat collins, c, 10 yrs   .254/.384
phil collins, rhp, 8 yrs   80/85 (with the phillies, so
                                             he can't be all bad)

roy collins, lhp, 7 yrs   89/62 and a 2.51 era!

and then you match it against:

eddie robinson, 1b, 13 yrs   .268/.439
jackie robinson, 2b, 10 yrs   .311/.474 (hall of fame)
yank robinson, ss, 10 yrs   .241/.323 (again a second
                                             baseman   with
                                             only 66 games
                                             at   short, but
                                             they—st.   louis,
                                             1885–89, had a
                                             guy named glea-
                                             son   at   short,
                                             who hit better)

brooks robinson, 3b   (still going—probable hall
                                     of fame)

frank robinson, of   (still going—possible hall of
                                     fame)

floyd robinson, of, 9 yrs   .283/.409
bill robinson, of   (still going—and he hits
                                     homeruns against the mets.
                                     he was called the black
                                     mickey mantle when he
                                     broke in with the yankees)

aaron robinson, c, 8 yrs   .260/.412
humberto robinson, rhp, 5 yrs   8/13 (an obvious weakness,
                                             but what can i do? at

least we'll score runs
to help him out)

hank robinson, 1hp, 6 yrs   41/37
wilbert robinson, utility and mgr. (our beloved uncle robbie—
                                        hall of fame)

that's a nice game, and if greg ever gets hold of a computer again i'll play them off. if you want you can try
with the jones or smiths or johnsons or millers and i'll
take you on. then there are the teams to screw up broad-
casters, like jones and john and johnson and johnston
and johnstone, etc. or the all-ski or all-zi teams. then i
had the all-time switch-hitting team, but got discouraged
because macmillan says that pete reiser only batted both
sides for 1948–51. markson swears it's wrong, but who
am i to argue?

but the best is to take off from say, cash, money, banks,
bonds, wes stock and push it until your catcher turns out
to have to be two guys platooned—gabby street and joe
"gummy" wall. okay?

one of the teams that seems to be obvious is the all-time
willies, but unfortunately that don't work out. you start
off great:

1b: mccovey
of: mays
of: keeler
of: stargall
of: reserve: davis, crawford, horton plus a couple of others
ss: miranda
3b: jones (pudd'nhead) or kamm
 p: carlton willey (and if you won't accept him there's always ramsdell, but then you're in trouble. no, willie jones did
play one game at second in his career, so i suppose we could
leave kamm on third and shift pudd'nhead, and we could al-

161

ways send stargall to the winter league for training as a catcher—or better yet we could put in willie dickey.)

you have more fun with the sibling teams. there's a lot of latitude there, but i have my ideal one, which is, in fact, a squad you could go through the season with, barring, like they say, injuries. the outfield is the dimaggios backed up by the alous, of course. i hate to ace out the waners but there were only two of them, even though they were pretty good. the infield has the boyers and the aspromontes, with cloyd boyer in the bullpen as pitching coach. the catchers are rick ferrell and walker cooper, so they can catch wes and mort, and the pitchers become a problem beause there are so many available. i have to go with the deans, the coveleskis, and christy mathewson and his brother henry. you could look it up. first base is, of course, hall-of-famer dan brouthers. sorry about that.

for a touch of local chauvinism i have to put in the all new york city team, to compete against all those southerners and midwesterners and californians that we think of as dominating the game. i'll play it against any geographical team you name:

1b: lou gehrig
2b: frankie frisch
3b: eddie yost
ss: phil rizzuto (only for new york would i let this yankee play for me—gehrig being only a dim memory to me, while this guy still hurts)
of: keeler
of: greenberg
of: colavito
 c: moe berg (there are probably better catchers from the city, but what other all-time team could moe make?)
 p: waite hoyt, sandy koufax, and whitey ford (i'm trying ford in the bullpen)

that's a nice team dredged up out of the bronx and queens and brooklyn and the sidewalks of manhattan. i think we needn't be ashamed.

i suppose it really is necessary for me to put in my all-jewish team. the idea's been beaten to death, and there's been plenty of laughs, but then one day my back got up, and by god, this ain't a bad team either:

1b: phil weintraub (.295 for 7 years, which is respectable)
2b: andy cohen (the giants' jewish hope, he wasn't terribly speedy)
ss: buddy myer (.303 lifetime, played second mostly but had over 200 games at short, so i moved him)
3b: goody rosen (of cleveland fame)
of: hank greenberg
of: sid gordon (in the encyclopedia of jews in sport it says he was the only man ever to pinchhit for mel ott. i don't believe it.)
of: lipman pike (the national league's homerun leader in 1877 with the grand total of 4)
 c: johnny kling (you could look him up too, for credentials)
 p: erskine mayer and sandy koufax

i'm fully aware that al shacht appears nowhere on this team. i said ballplayers.

the last team i worked out came out of dave markson's fertile but slightly sick imagination—he was envisioning what the old-timers' games were coming to and finally postulated the all-time tragedy team, with the disasters to be reenacted in yankee stadium one sunny day for everyone's edification. david and i started it, but i have to admit that we had to call supersleuth don honig in; everyone needs someone like don around, with a steel-trap memory for names, averages, trivia. he supplied us with short and third:

1b: eddie waitkus (shot by the girl who was mad at her father)

2b: kennie hubbs (after a fantastic start, killed himself crashing a light plane into a cornfield)

ss: ray chapman (not only hit by a pitched ball, but killed by it)

3b: eddie grant (killed in action, the argonne forest, a month before the armistice in world war i)

of: pete reiser (bouncing off walls before they were rubberized)

of: joe medwick (and god only knows how high his average would've been before he got beaned)

of: shoeless joe jackson (ruined in the black sox scandal and, seemingly, an innocent dupe)

catcher is a tough one, between roy campanella's car accident and willard herschberger committing suicide in a boston hotel room because he dropped a foul pop. you pick.

and for pitching, again a three-man staff, with dean losing his motion because of a line drive off the toes, score losing his eyes with another line drive, and monte stratton shooting his toes off in a hunting accident. i beg you to believe that the game can be played endlessly if the need is there. how about guys named joe?

Like, i just decided to check out george wright, stellar shortstop of the 1870's. he was born in yonkers! is there a team there? last i remember was a short-lived thing either during or after the war called the yonkers chiefs, which used to draw about twelve fans. but supposing—supposing there is a catcher from yonkers, by god, there may be a team.

THINGS I CAN'T DO AT SHEA STADIUM

eat peanuts with no teeth;
drink beer, on the wagon;
order sandwiches, too goyishe;
stand the sodas, too sweet;
eat before i go, which means i have
to eat two hotdogs which aren't
very good; cheer a good player
on the other side if there's
any possibility of him hurting
us; pay absolute attention to
every play; open the out door
from the outside or the in door
from the inside in the johns,
nobody can; stand heights, i
think i'll fall into center
field; yell unselfconsciously
to "get a bingle" during a
rally, or to start one off;
accept losing; accept winning.